TIME

Grammar, Usage, & Mechanics

By the Editors of TIME Learning Ventures

Teacher Created Materials
PUBLISHING

TIME
Grammar, Usage, and Mechanics
Secondary Level
Copyright © 2006
Time Inc.

TIME Learning Ventures
Editorial Director: Keith Garton
Editor: Jonathan Rosenbloom
Project Editor: Jennifer Nissenbaum,
    Baseline Development Group
Design Production: Derrick Alderman & Jennifer Brown,
    Dinardo Design
Illustrator: Kathryn Adams
Teacher Reviewers: Brian Glassman, MD; Nancy Kern, VA;
    Vincent LaRuina, NY; Greg Matchett, AZ;
    Jana Miller, TX; JoAnne Winnick, CA

Exploring Writing™
Copyright © 2006
Teacher Created Materials Publishing

Teacher Created Materials
Publisher: Rachelle Cracchiolo, M.S. Ed.
Editor in Chief: Sharon Coan, M.S. Ed.
Editorial Project Manager: Dona Herweck Rice

ISBN: 0-7439-0132-0

Teacher Created
Materials Publishing
5301 Oceanus Drive
Huntington Beach, CA 92649
www.tcmpub.com

Photography Credits
Page 1: Comstock; Page 9: Photodisc; Page 10: Courtesy Metropolitan Opera; Page 15: Don Heupel/AP Wide World; Page 16: Photodisc; Page 20: Photodisc; Page 21: Comstock; Page 23: Photodisc; Page 28: Michael A. Mariant/AP Wide World; Page 29: Photodisc; Page 32: Royalty-Free/Corbis; Page 33: Brand X Pictures/Punchstock; Page 38: Jennifer Graylock/AP Wide World; Page 46: Comstock; Page 52: Johner/Getty Images; Page 53: AP Wide World; Page 54: AP Wide World; Page 56: Jonik/Wikimedia Commons; Page 60: Comstock; Page 64: Photodisc; Page 65: Comstock; Page 67: Comstock; Page 71: Photodisc

Grammar, Usage, & Mechanics

• •

©TIME Inc.

#10132

©TIME Inc.

Name _____   Date _____

Kinds of Sentences

A **sentence** is a group of words that expresses a complete thought. Sentences begin with a capital letter, have a subject and a predicate, and are classified as **declarative, interrogative, imperative,** or **exclamatory** based on their content.

• •

A **declarative sentence** makes a statement and ends with a period.

> The tomatoes in our garden are ripening**.**

• •

An **interrogative sentence** asks a question and ends with a question mark.

> Should we pick the red ones this morning**?**

• •

An **imperative sentence** gives a command or makes a request and ends with a period.

> Do not pick the green ones**.**   Please pull that weed**.**

• •

An **exclamatory sentence** expresses urgency, excitement, or a strong feeling and ends with an exclamation point.

> Ooh**!** I found a worm**!**   Watch out for that snake**!**

• •

❶ Show What You Know

Label each sentence below as declarative, interrogative, imperative, or exclamatory.

We have worked many hours in this vegetable garden.   _____

This zucchini is just enormous!   _____

Please buy more jars for canning today.   _____

Should we plant more corn next year?   _____

Name _____ Date _____

❷ Take It Up a Notch

Label each sentence in the paragraph below as either declarative, interrogative, imperative, or exclamatory.

Years ago, at the end of the summer, families with gardens made preparations

to store the vegetables and fruits that they would eat all winter long. _____

What hard work it was! _____ Safely storing the produce required

sterilizing jars in hot water and much paring and chopping. _____

Not many people can their own vegetables and fruits these days, but my great-aunt Mae

still does. _____ I helped her yesterday. _____

The kitchen was so hot that I thought I would faint! _____

"If we are putting the beans in jars," I asked my great-aunt Mae, "why is it called 'canning'?"

_____ She did not know the answer. _____

Where will I find the answer to my question? _____

• •

❸ On Your Own

Now it is time for a research project. Your task is simple: Count and record how many of the four kinds of sentences there are in two of your favorite books. Make a tally sheet with four columns, one for each kind of sentence. Open the first book to a full page of text and begin reading. Each time you come to the end of a sentence, decide what kind of sentence it is and put a mark in the appropriate column. What is the most and least common kind of sentence on that page? Now open the second book and start your tally. How do the two compare? Record your findings in a short paragraph.

Editors' Tips from TIME

✔ When we compose an informal e-mail to a friend, we might find ourselves writing many exclamatory sentences, filling our message with exclamation points. That kind of message can be fun to send and fun to receive, but if you use too many exclamatory sentences in a more formal piece of writing, the reader might become distracted from the point of your message. Remember that in formal writing, true exclamatory sentences should be rare. When exclamation points are overused, they lose their impact!

   #10132   ©TIME Inc.

Name _____ Date _____

Simple Subjects and Predicates

A complete sentence has a **subject** that tells the reader *who* or *what* is being described and a **predicate** that indicates what the subject of the sentence *does* or *is*.

• •

A **simple subject** is the main word or words of the subject. A **simple predicate** is the main word or words of the predicate. A simple predicate is always a verb, meaning it is a word showing action or being.

simple subject   simple predicate

The red **radio** on Darla's nightstand suddenly **blared** her favorite song.

• •

In an imperative sentence, the subject may be stated; however, most often it is not stated since it is understood to be the pronoun *you*. In the first sentence, the reader is left to infer that the subject is *you*.

predicate   subject predicate

Please lower the volume.   **You** lower the volume.

• •

To find the subject of some interrogative sentences, you might find it helpful to rearrange the sentence and change it from a question to a statement.

simple predicate simple subject   simple subject simple predicate

Was **Jack** at the party?   **Jack** was at the party.

• •

❶ Show What You Know

Circle the simple subject and underline the simple predicate in each sentence.

My sister bought new curtains for her bedroom.

The blue curtains match her bedspread.

Above her desk, she hung a new poster.

It shows her favorite band in front of the Statue of Liberty.

She arranged her books alphabetically in a bookcase.

Go on

Name _____ Date _____

❷ Take It Up a Notch

Circle the simple subjects and underline the simple predicates in the paragraph below.

My bedroom is down the hall from my sister's. In my room, many trophies stand on the

bureau. Pictures of my favorite football players hang on the walls. The accomplishments

of those players inspire me. On the shelf above my desk, I keep my books. The biography

of Doug Flutie is my favorite one. Have you ever read it? You should read it. My room is

quiet and private. Privacy is important to me. An immaculate room is not important to me.

Yesterday, for the first time in weeks, I ran the vacuum cleaner in my room. That old

machine is noisy and heavy. The dust bunnies under my bed ran for their lives!

❸ On Your Own

Write a paragraph about your favorite room at home. The paragraph could describe
your bedroom or the room where you play your drums or do something else for fun.
Describe the room in detail. Write about the things you like to do there. Then, go back
and circle the subject and underline the predicate of each sentence.

Editors' Tips from TIME

✔ Readers like variety. It keeps them interested in what they are reading. One way to
give readers what they like is to vary your sentence structure. Remember that the
subject of a sentence does not always have to be at the very beginning. You might
use an introductory word or phrase to begin a sentence.

Name _____ Date _____

Compound Subjects and Predicates

A **compound subject** is made up of two or more simple subjects connected by *and, or, either . . . or,* or *neither . . . nor.*

> **Jenna** *and* **Kyle** want to play on a team at school this year.
>
> Every fall, *either* a **coach** *or* a **manager** talks to kids about tryouts.
>
> *Neither* **track** *nor* **rugby** is popular at our school.

• •

A **compound predicate** is made up of two or more simple predicates connected by *and, or, either . . . or,* or *neither . . . nor.*

> The coach **claps** *and* **cheers** for the players as they leave the field.
>
> The ball *either* **falls** through the hoop *or* **bounces** off the rim.
>
> You must *neither* **miss** a practice *nor* **arrive** late for a game.

• •

When a **compound subject** or a **compound predicate** contains more than two elements, use a comma between the elements and before the conjunctions *and* and *or.*

> Special pads**,** shoes**,** *and* helmets are required.
>
> To be in shape, you must eat right**,** sleep well**,** *and* exercise regularly.
>
> You may try out for soccer**,** football**,** baseball**,** *or* tennis.

• •

❶ Show What You Know

Underline the compound subjects and predicates below.

Croquet and badminton are games a family can play in the backyard.

Wooden balls, mallets, and wire wickets are the required equipment for croquet.

A net, rackets, and a birdie make up the equipment for badminton.

The Farquar family and the Feeble family challenged each other to a game of croquet.

Kyle and Jenna yelled and hooted for both family teams.

Neither Mr. Feeble nor Mr. Farquar had played croquet before.

At first, the Farquars fumbled and flailed, but they triumphed in the end.

Go on

Name _____ Date _____

❷ Take It Up a Notch

In the letter below, underline each subject in a compound subject and each predicate in a compound predicate. Circle the connecting words.

Dear Ms. Dymkowski:

I would like to apply for the position of junior coach-in-training for the peewee soccer team. I have trained and coached both of my little brothers in baseball. They understand and love the game because I made it fun to learn. Although I have never coached soccer, my sister and I have been playing the game since we were six years old. Of course, coordination and flexibility are important things to develop in young players. Team spirit and self-confidence are even more important. On the playing field, neither timid children nor inexperienced children should feel left out. A good junior coach-in-training should support and help less-skilled players to enjoy the sport. Coach Rice, Coach Salonpuro, and Coach Ayers have agreed to recommend me for the position. I hope to hear from you soon.

Sincerely,

Jenna Kaufman

• •

❸ On Your Own

With a partner, make a list of five possible compound subjects and five possible compound predicates. Exchange lists and write ten sentences based on your partner's list. To make the activity more fun, base your list on a silly theme that will challenge your partner to write funny sentences.

Editors' Tips from TIME

✔ When you are proofreading your work, watch for *either . . . or* and *neither . . . nor* in your compound subjects and predicates. Be sure that you have included both parts of these connectors correctly and that you have not used the first part of one with the second part of the other. In other words, do not combine *either . . . nor* or *neither . . . or*.

Name _____ Date _____

Sentence Fragments and Run-on Sentences

A **sentence fragment** is an unfinished sentence written as if it were a full sentence. Often a fragment can be corrected by connecting it to the previous sentence.

Fragment: Mozart composed many pieces of music. **For the piano and other instruments.**

Revision: Mozart composed many pieces of music for the piano and other instruments.

• •

Sometimes you can make a fragment into a full sentence by adding a missing element.

Fragment: Kelly has improved her technique. **Practicing every day.**

Revision: Kelly has improved her technique <u>by</u> **practicing every day.**

• •

A **run-on sentence** is two or more sentences joined together as if they were one sentence. A run-on sentence happens when two independent clauses are joined by only a comma or are run together without any punctuation. Separate the sentences into two simple sentences or add a conjunction and the correct punctuation to form a compound sentence.

Run-on: Clyde is taking trumpet lessons**,** **he** likes the sound of that instrument.

Revision: Clyde is taking trumpet lessons**.** **He** likes the sound of that instrument.

Alternate revision: Clyde is taking trumpet lessons **because** he likes the sound of that instrument.

• •

❶ Show What You Know

Examine each example below to determine whether it is a fragment, a run-on, or a sentence. Write your conclusion on the line at the end of the example.

The music program at our school is one of the best in the state. _____

The altos singing the melody in the second verse of that piece. _____

Ms Bruno has a conductor's baton she will begin the concert soon. _____

Since I want to play in the high school marching band. _____

Because the song has a good beat. _____

In the band that practices here on Tuesday. _____

If the band's bus arrives on time, I'll be surprised I'll be happy, too. _____

Go on

Name _____ Date _____

❷ Take It Up a Notch

For each run-on or sentence fragment below, compose a complete sentence.

I started taking piano lessons seven years ago. When I was only six years old.

_____

I had to learn to read music, that was easier than I thought it would be.

_____

I learned how long to hold each kind of note. Counting all the time.

_____

My teacher taught me a rhyme about the names of the lines and spaces, it was easy and fun.

_____

✔ Proofreading Power!

Using the appropriate proofreader's marks shown in the box, find and correct the seven mistakes in this concert review.

The Shelbyville Community Band concert took place on the town common last night. The concert opened with "Tune for a Turtle" by Ima Slowmover? Naturally, the tempo was slow! Next, the Twitchel twins played their piece with silver spoons and drinking glasses filled with water. Twyla either gently tapped nor roughly banged the spoons on her knee. While her brother ran a wet finger around the rims of the glasses. Neither twyla or her brother Twane missed a beat. At the end of the concert, the entire band joined in a rousing rendition of Mr. Tabby's "Meow Melody." Which brought the crowd to its feet.

¶	Indent paragraph
⌃	Add
⊙	Add a period
℘	Delete
☰	Capitalize
/	Make lowercase
∽	Reverse

Name _____ Date _____

Nouns

A **common noun** is a word that names a person, place, thing, or idea. When a noun names an idea, it names something that cannot be touched or seen. A **proper noun** names a particular person, place, thing, or idea. Proper nouns begin with capital letters. When a proper noun consists of more than one word, capitalize only the important words.

>   **S**tatue of **L**iberty   **A**venue of the **A**mericas   **M**anhattan **S**chool of **M**usic

• •

A **singular noun** names one person, place, thing, or idea, and a **plural noun** names more than one. To form the plurals of most nouns, add −s to the singular. Some nouns follow other patterns. Look at the ending of a singular noun to help you decide how to form the plural.

Forming Plural Nouns: *When a noun ends with . . .*	
−z, −s, −x, −ch, or −sh	**add −es**
a vowel and −y	**add −s, usually**
a consonant and −y	**change the −y to −i and add −es**
−f or −fe	**add −s to some nouns and change the −f to −v and add −es for others**
a vowel and −o	**add −s**
a consonant and −o	**add −s to some nouns and −es to others**

• •

Some nouns do not follow the above rules. They have irregular plural forms.

>   child ⟶ **children**   foot ⟶ **feet**   goose ⟶ **geese**

Others have the same form in the plural as they do in the singular.

>   moose   sheep   species   salmon   series

• •

❶ Show What You Know

Underline the common nouns in the paragraph below and double underline the proper nouns. Label each noun as either *s* for singular or *p* for plural.

People ride the subway every day in New York City. The system is quite complicated,

but generally it runs well. The map at the entrance shows lines of various colors

crossing each other. Visitors to the city are often confused, but I will act as your

guide. Here comes our train. Hop aboard the Metropolitan Transit Authority!

Name _____ Date _____

❷ Take It Up a Notch

Circle the correct form of the underlined noun in the sentences below.

When we arrived at <u>Lincoln center/Lincoln Center</u>, our <u>group/Group</u> went directly

to the <u>lobby/Lobby</u> of the building where the <u>metropolitan Opera/Metropolitan Opera</u>

performs. In the lobby, we saw two stunning <u>murals/Murals</u>

by the <u>artist/Artist</u> <u>marc chagall/Marc Chagall</u>. Of all the

theater <u>lobbys/lobbies</u> I've ever seen, this one is the most

impressive. Chagall's work towers over its <u>viewers/vieweres</u>.

The younger <u>childs/children</u> in our tour group asked to be

lifted up to better see the <u>Works of Art/works of art</u>. Our

tour guide explained that Chagall drew his inspiration from

the <u>storys/stories</u> and Jewish folklore that he heard in his

childhood. The murals are full of bright <u>colores/colors</u> and

magical floating figures. I wonder how many <u>foots/feet</u> tall

the murals are.

Marc Chagall, *The Triumph of Music*

• •

❸ On Your Own

Working with a partner, write a quiz containing a list of singular nouns that includes at least
one noun from each of the categories on page 9. Be sure to include nouns that have not
been used in this lesson. Check a dictionary to be sure you know how the plurals should
be spelled before you hand out your quiz. Now challenge a pair of your classmates to write
the correct plural forms of the nouns. Then take a quiz that another group wrote.

Editors' Tips from TIME

✔ When a singular noun ends in a consonant followed by *-o*, it can be tricky to pluralize
   because of variations in usage. The preferred plural for *potato* is *potatoes*, but the
   plural of *zero* can be spelled either *zeros* or *zeroes*. As with any question about spelling,
   it is best to check a dictionary to be sure that you are using an acceptable spelling.

Name _____ Date _____

Collective Nouns

A **collective noun** names a group of people, animals, or things. Collective nouns pose a challenge for writers because the singular form of a collective noun may take a singular verb in some instances and a plural verb in others. When the collective noun refers to a group that is acting as a whole, it takes a singular verb. When the group's members act individually, the collective noun takes a plural verb.

Singular	Plural
The **band** plays every Saturday.	The members of the **band** have all left.
The **crowd** cheers loudly.	The peoplein the **crowd** are clapping.

When a collective noun refers to a group acting as one unit, use a singular pronoun to refer to it. When the collective noun refers to members of the group acting as individuals, use a plural pronoun.

Singular	Plural
The **jury** reaches its verdict.	The **jury** members reach for their coats.
The **family** enjoys its dinner.	The **family** members post their schedules.

❶ Show What You Know

Underline the collective nouns below. Label singular collectives with an s and plural collectives with a p.

School athletics is the topic of conversation at the meeting.

A group of students offers a demonstration of karate.

The audience stand or lean forward in their seats.

The furniture has been moved out of the way.

A flock of birds gathers in the tree outside the window to watch.

The group reach for their pencils or pens.

The committee votes to offer a karate class to students next year.

Go on

Name _____ Date _____

❷ Take It Up a Notch

**Decide whether the collective noun in each sentence
is singular or plural. Label the collective noun and
circle the correct form of the verb and the correct pronoun.**

A flock _____ of geese (flies/fly) over the school.

Our school's faculty _____ (meets/meet) every Wednesday.

The faculty _____ (is/are) experts in (its/their) fields.

The team _____ (practices/practice) for (its/their) final game.

At the buzzer, the entire crowd _____ in the gym (rises/rise) to (its/their) feet.

The couple _____ in the first row (leaves/leave) early.

The family _____ (disagrees/disagree) on some of the referee's calls.

An army _____ of sports reporters (invades/invade) the locker room.

• •

❸ On Your Own

We all know that a group of cows is called a *herd* and that a group of bees is called a
swarm, but few people know that a group of ravens is called an *unkindness* of ravens.
There are other quite unusual names for groups of creatures. See how many you can
learn by doing some research on the Internet. Compare your list with a friend's list.

Editors' Tips from TIME

✔ Sometimes, even when it is correct, a plural verb just "sounds wrong" to our ears.
When this is the case, try revising the sentence to avoid the problem. For instance,
The committee arrive at varying conclusions could be rewritten as *The committee
members arrive at varying conclusions.* If you please your own ear, you will probably
please your reader's ear, too.

©TIME Inc.

Name _____ Date _____

Compound Nouns

A **compound noun** is a noun made up of two or more words. There are three kinds of compound nouns: solid compounds, hyphenated compounds, and open compounds.

Solid compounds:	teacup	textbook	lightbulb
Hyphenated compounds:	sister-in-law	runner-up	walkie-talkie
Open compounds:	high school	hair stylist	social worker

Form the plural of a solid compound noun as you would any other noun.

teacup**s**   textbook**s**   lunchbox**es**

Form the plural of hyphenated and open compounds by adding the appropriate ending to the most important word in the compound.

sister**s**-in-law   runner**s**-up   social worker**s**

Form the possessive of a compound noun by adding an apostrophe and an −s to the last word in the compound.

lightbulb**'s**   sister-in-law**'s**   high school**'s**

When you are forming the plural possessive of a compound noun, first follow the rule for forming the plural and then the rule for forming the possessive.

sister**s**-in-law**'s**   textbook**s'**   hair stylist**s'**

❶ Show What You Know

Circle the compound nouns below. Label the noun with an s if it is singular and a p if it is plural. If it is possessive, add pos to your label.

The middle school will have elections next month.   _____

Students in all the homerooms vote for the officers.   _____

Cynthia is running for the office of secretary-treasurer.   _____

Each class will elect a president and two vice presidents.   _____

The vice presidents' duties will be divided according to the school's constitution.   _____

Go on

Name _____ Date _____

❷ Take It Up a Notch

**Form the singular possessive, the plural, and the plural possessive
of each compound noun in the list below.**

Compound Noun	Singular Possessive	Plural	Plural Possessive
weekend	_____	_____	_____
parking meter	_____	_____	_____
father-in-law	_____	_____	_____
hair stylist	_____	_____	_____
Web page	_____	_____	_____
secretary-general	_____	_____	_____
video game	_____	_____	_____

• •

❸ On Your Own

Working with a small group, draft a list of all the compound nouns that you can think of.
You might not be sure if you should use a hyphen in the compound, join the words without
a hyphen, or write them as separate words. You might not even be sure if the words form
a real compound noun! This is when a dictionary comes in handy. After you make a draft
of your list, appoint a member of your group to check each entry in a dictionary. Appoint
another member to make any corrections as you go. Gather all the lists from the groups
and make a class list of compound nouns that all students can refer to when writing.

Editors' Tips from TIME

✔ How does a writer decide whether a compound noun should be written in a solid
form, a hyphenated form, or an open form? This question is best answered by
referring to a recently published dictionary. Many compounds that were first written
in the open form or in a hyphenated form have come, over time, to be written in the
solid form because readers now easily recognize them that way. Remembering that
you want to use the form that your audience will most easily read and understand
will help you decide which form of compound noun to use.

Name _____   Date _____

Possessive Nouns

A **possessive noun** names the *who* or *what* that possesses or owns something.
Form the possessive of a singular noun by adding an apostrophe and an *–s*.

> **team's** colors   **buffalo's** hide   Mr. **Hoss's** ticket   **Doug Flutie's** helmet

Form the possessive of a plural noun that ends in *–s* by placing an apostrophe after the final
–s of the word.

> **players'** bus   **babies'** cries   **boys'** uniforms   **glasses'** contents

Form the possessive of a plural noun that does not end in *–s* by adding an apostrophe and
an *–s*.

> **men's** shoes   **people's** cheers   **geese's** honks   **media's** coverage

If there are two or more owners who possess the same thing, use the correct possessive
form only for the noun closest to the thing possessed.

> Mitch and **Charlie's** team   Bob and his **sons'** cheers

❶ Show What You Know

**Underline the possessive nouns in the sentences below
and label them with an s for singular or a *p* for plural.**

Doug Flutie's home state is Maryland, but he has long been a
favorite football player of that sport's fans in Massachusetts.
On the day after Thanksgiving in 1984, he captured Boston
College fans' hearts when he threw the game's amazing final
pass with only six seconds remaining on the clock. The team's
win against the University of Miami was one for the record
books, and that day's performance helped Doug Flutie win
college football's most coveted award, the Heisman Trophy.

Doug Flutie

Name _____ Date _____

❷ Take It Up a Notch

Fill in the blanks with the possessive form of the noun.

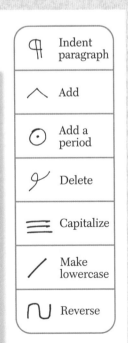

Doug and his wife Laurie have two children, Alexa and Douglas Jr. _____ son,

Doug and Laurie

who is called Dougie, suffers from a disorder known as autism. _____ symptoms

autism

may include difficulty with expressing needs, little eye contact, and resistance to change.

An _____ symptoms can vary from mild to severe. _____

individual   **Doug Flutie Jr.**

symptoms first appeared when he was about three years old. The _____ response

Flutie family

to their _____ diagnosis of autism has helped not only Dougie but also other

son

children and their families. The Fluties formed the Douglas Flutie Jr. Foundation for Autism.

The _____ mission is to help families who are living with _____

foundation   **autism**

challenges. Now Dougie attends school and benefits from a _____ help as well.

tutor

Proofreading Power!

**Using the proofreader's marks shown in the box,
correct the eight errors in the paragraph below.**

My familys favorite sport is football. Going to the high school's
games in our hometown is my mother's and father's favorite Friday
night activity. The team have a game this weekend. It should be a
tough game because our opponents record is three wins and no
losses so far. Our team has a good record too, and our defensive
and offensive coach's is confident. The coaches main concern
is the health of the players. Everyone hopes that the quarterbacks'
ankle has healed since the last game.

¶	Indent paragraph
⌄	Add
⊙	Add a period
⌿	Delete
＝	Capitalize
/	Make lowercase
∩	Reverse

©TIME Inc.

Name _____ Date _____

Kinds of Verbs

There are two **kinds of verbs: action verbs** and **verbs of being.** An action verb tells what the subject does or what is done to it. A verb of being expresses the status or condition of the subject. The verb in a sentence can also express time and duration, depending on its tense. A verb must always agree with its subject in number and person.

Action verbs: David **sent** an invitation to everyone in the class.

My friends **shop** for new clothes to wear to the party.

Verbs of being: Everyone **is** excited about the celebration.

David **feels** confident about the decorations.

· ·

The most common verb of being is the verb *to be.*

Present tense of the verb *to be*	
Singular	*Plural*
I am	we are
you are	you are

Present tense of the verb *to be*	
Singular	*Plural*
she or he is	they are
it is	they are

· ·

Verbs of being frequently link the subject of a sentence to another word in the predicate. This is sometimes called a linking verb. Some common linking verbs are *to seem, to become, to look, to appear, to feel, to taste, to smell.* Some of these verbs may also be action verbs.

As a verb of being: That popcorn *smells* great!

As an action verb: David *smells* the pizza burning.

· ·

❶ Show What You Know

Circle the verbs of being and underline the action verbs.

David chooses the music for tonight's event. Aki is in charge of the CD player, and he plays a variety of songs. Some guests knock on the back door. The pizza tastes good, and the colas are cold. Almost everyone moves when the music starts. David dashes upstairs for more potato chips. What a great party!

Go on

Name _____ Date _____

❷ Take It Up a Notch

Fill in each blank in the paragraph below with either an action verb or a verb of being. Use the present tense and be sure that the verb agrees in number with its noun. Choose verbs that make the story lively and vivid.

The party guests _____ at the back door of David's house. Inside, the music

_____ loudly. The bass notes _____ , and the singer

_____ . The guests _____ over the din. Jim _____

Alice to dance. For a while, Denny _____ the couple. Jim _____

his arms and _____ his feet while Alice _____ and

_____ . Denny _____ Alice more than any other girl at the party,

but he _____ shy. He _____ pizza and _____ root

beer. Jim and Alice and the other dancers _____ . Denny _____

miserable, but finally the music _____ . Alice _____ toward

Denny. His hands _____ sweaty and his heart _____ . "Hi,"

_____ Alice to the nervous boy, "let's dance."

• •

❸ On Your Own

What is your favorite activity? Is it dancing, playing music, reading, or playing sports such as football, baseball, or Ping-Pong? Make a list of all the action verbs you can think of that you might use in a story about what you like to do best. Then write a story using at least four different action verbs and at least two different verbs of being. Read your story aloud to a friend. Do the verbs you have chosen convey the excitement or the enjoyment you want a reader to feel?

Editors' Tips from TIME

✔ Sometimes writers use too many descriptive words in an attempt to make their stories more exciting or interesting to readers. When you're writing, stop and think of a verb that will give your reader a vivid picture in a simple statement. For instance, instead of writing "said loudly," you might write "yelled."

Name _____ Date _____

Transitive and Intransitive Verbs

A **transitive verb** expresses action that is directed toward a noun or pronoun.
That noun or pronoun is called the **direct object.**

transitive verb   direct object

Dale **arranges** the toast on a plate.

• •

A transitive verb may also be followed by a word that tells *to whom* or *to what* the action
is done. This word is called an **indirect object.**

transitive verb   indirect object

Dale **passes** Paula the plate.

• •

An **intransitive verb** expresses an action that is not directed toward an object. An
intransitive verb may be followed by an adverb or a group of words acting as an adverb.
Verbs of being are always intransitive and may by followed by a subject complement.

intransitive verb   adverbial phrase   verb of being   subject complement

The innkeepers **bustle** around the kitchen.   They **are** busy.

• •

Some verbs, such as *hit* and *climb,* are only transitive. Other verbs, such as *sleep* and *fall,*
are only intransitive. But some verbs can be both.

transitive verb   direct object   intransitive verb   adverbial phrase

Transitive: Dale **studied** the cookbook.   **Intransitive:** He **studied** for an hour.

• •

❶ Show What You Know

**Underline each transitive verb and draw an arrow pointing
to its direct object. Circle the intransitive verbs.**

The inn's guests gather around the breakfast table.

Today's menu includes blueberry pancakes.

Paula pours coffee into the delicate china cups.

Paula and Dale Williams graduated from the Institute of Hospitality.

They opened the Wildlife Lodge last year.

Go on

Name _____   Date _____

❷ Take It Up a Notch

Dale and Paula have written the following paragraph to be included in an advertisement for their inn. Label the underlined verbs with a *t* for transitive or an *i* for intransitive. If the verb is transitive, label its direct object with *do*.

If you are looking for a rustic yet elegant retreat, the Wildlife Lodge <u>is</u> for you.

When you arrive at the lodge, Barney, the resident dog, <u>comes</u> to the door

with his tail wagging. Dale and Paula, Barney's assistants, <u>carry</u> your bags

to one of the lodge's comfortable rooms. Each room in the lodge <u>is</u>

<u>decorated</u> charmingly. Watercolors of local wildlife <u>hang</u> on the walls.

Paula, an accomplished decorator and artist, <u>painted</u> each one herself.

The kitchen <u>is</u> Dale's territory. Dale <u>cooks</u> breakfast every morning.

He has <u>perfected</u> a secret recipe for flapjacks. Dale, Paula, and Barney

look forward to making your stay at Wildlife Lodge a pleasant one.

• •

❸ On Your Own

Make a list of verbs that are not used in this lesson. Include in your list both action verbs and verbs of being or condition. Now write a sentence for each verb. Is the verb in that sentence acting as a transitive or an intransitive verb? If the verb is transitive, try writing another sentence in which that same verb is intransitive. If the verb is intransitive, try writing another sentence in which the verb is transitive. Which of the verbs on your list can only be transitive? Which of the verbs can only be intransitive?

Editors' Tips from TIME

✔ Usually, transitive verbs need direct objects to complete their meanings. Technically, a sentence is complete when it contains a subject and a verb. Upon reading the sentence *Sherman catches*, however, the reader might ask, "What does Sherman catch?" Does he catch a robber, the measles, or a baseball? The answer can be discovered when the sentence is considered in context. *The players take the field. Kelly pitches. Sherman catches.*

Name _____   Date _____

Verb Phrases

When a group of two or more words acts as a verb, it is called a **verb phrase.** A verb phrase is made up of a **main verb,** which shows action or being, and an **auxiliary verb,** which works with the main verb. There may be more than one auxiliary verb in a verb phrase. A verb phrase follows this pattern: auxiliary verb + main verb. There may be other words between the auxiliary verb and the main verb.

Sentences with Verb Phrases	Auxiliary Verb(s)	Main Verb
Bats **are hanging** in the cave.	are	hanging
I **am** not **afraid** of bats.	am	afraid
By nightfall, they **will have eaten** many flying insects.	will have	eaten

• •

The contraction for *not* may be attached to some auxiliary verbs, and some auxiliary verbs can be contracted.

Manny did **not** pack a lunch.   Manny did**n't** pack a lunch.

He should **have** thought ahead.   He should**'ve** thought ahead.

• •

Sometimes a verb that acts as an auxiliary verb in one sentence may act as a main verb in another sentence.

She **has** pitched the tent under a tree.   has = auxiliary verb

Carla **has** a pair of binoculars.   has = main verb

• •

❶ Show What You Know

Underline the verb phrases in the paragraph below. Label the main verbs with *mv* and the auxiliary verbs with *av.*

Yuri and Megan are hiking in the woods with Dr. Phoebe Truax. For many years, Dr. Truax

has been teaching botany, a course on the biology of plants, at the university. She knows

more about endangered varieties of plants than anyone else in the world. "I've never seen

such beautiful lady's slippers," she says. Dr. Truax is kneeling in the grass and is cradling

a delicate pink blossom in her hand. "This plant has been endangered for many

years." Yuri and Megan are recording what they find in their nature journals.

Go on ➡

Name _____ Date _____

❷ Take It Up a Notch

Here is Yuri's journal entry from his nature hike. Fill in the auxiliary verb or verbs missing from each verb phrase. Circle the entire verb phrase.

Megan and I _____ just returned from a hike with Dr. Truax, the famous

botanist. I _____ never _____ known that there are endangered

plants in our local forest if we _____ not hiked with Dr. Truax. She is amazingly

knowledgeable! The lady's slipper was our most exciting find. (I _____ drawn

a sketch of it on the previous page.) I _____ remember the spot where we

found that endangered plant and return soon. After we found the lady's slipper, we

_____ walking along a shaded path where I noticed some low plants with

dark green leaves and red berries. By mistake, I stepped on

a few of the plants and _____ startled by a faint

smell of mint. Dr. Truax told us the plant _____

called wintergreen. The candies in my pocket _____

called wintergreen mints!

❸ On Your Own

Look at a page from a piece of fiction. Read each sentence closely and make a list of
any verb phrases you find on a separate sheet of paper. How many different auxiliary
verbs did you find on that one page of text?

Editors' Tips from TIME

✔ Choosing the correct auxiliary verb is crucial for communicating time and sequence in
your writing. Reading your composition out loud may help you decide whether or not
you have chosen the right auxiliary verbs. Your ear may tell you when you have made a
mistake because choosing the correct auxiliary verb when speaking often comes more
naturally than when writing.

Name _____ Date _____

Verb Tenses

The tense of a verb tells us how the action or state of being relates to time. There are six **verb tenses** in English: three simple tenses and three perfect tenses. The simple tenses—past (*called*), present (*call*), and future (*will call*)—are most common. The perfect tenses—present perfect, past perfect, and future perfect—need auxiliary verbs. The past participle is a verb form used with *have, has,* or *had* to form the perfect tense. The present tense, the past tense, and the past participle are the principal parts of a verb: *call, called, called.*

• •

Use the **present perfect** tense for an action that was begun in the past and was completed at an unspecified time or that continues in the present. The present perfect is formed by combining the present tense form of the auxiliary verb *have* with the past participle of the main verb.

> War **has left** its mark on Britain.

> For years, tourists **have flocked** to the Tower of London.

• •

Use the **past perfect** tense for actions completed by a specific time in the past or actions completed before some other past action occurred. The past perfect is formed by combining the auxiliary verb *had* with the past participle of the main verb.

> Herman **had eaten** three crumpets by the time I finished my milk.

• •

Use the **future perfect** tense for an action that will be completed by a specific time in the future. Form the future perfect tense by combining the auxiliary verbs *shall have* or *will have* with the past participle of the main verb.

> By the end of the week, the tour group **will have visited** six museums.

• •

❶ Show What You Know

Underline the verb or verb phrase, and label each sentence according to its verb tense.

Our tour group will meet at the airport tomorrow afternoon.   _____

I packed my suitcase three days ago.   _____

I always plan ahead for long trips.   _____

I had repacked my suitcase three times before noon.   _____

Now we are all together at the airport.   _____

Go on ➡

Name _____ Date _____

❷ Take It Up a Notch

Fill in the blanks with the correct form of the verb in parentheses.

The Tower of London *(to stand)* _____ for over 900 years. The site *(to be)*

_____ one of the most popular tourist attractions in the city. Visitors to the

Tower *(to view)* _____ the spectacular crown jewels and *(to hear)*

_____ about the bloody history of the place. By the time you exit the grounds

today, you *(to hear)* _____ about the tragic last days of Anne Boleyn, Lady Jane

Grey, Sir Walter Raleigh, and other Londoners who were once imprisoned here. Yesterday,

you *(to see)* _____ a number of beautiful churches. In a short while, you *(to see)*

_____ St. John's Chapel, which is a beautiful part of this immense building.

One curious part of the history of the Tower has to do with some large black birds. At least

six ravens *(to live)* _____ in the Tower since the days of King Charles II.

Legend has it that if the ravens leave, the Tower of London *(to fall)* _____.

• •

❸ On Your Own

Write an account of a trip that you have taken. Use each
of the six verb tenses at least once in your story. Underline
and label the verb or verb phrase in each sentence.

Editors' Tips from TIME

✔ Have you ever noticed that people sometimes use the present tense to talk about
an event that happened in the past? For instance, you may hear the narrator of a
historical film say, "In December 1941, Congress **declares** war." The speaker is using
what is called the historical present. Everyone understands that the event took place
in the past, but the speaker chooses to use the present tense to add a sense of drama
and immediacy.

Name _____ Date _____

Progressive Forms of Verbs

Each of the six verb tenses has a **progressive form.** The progressive verb forms describe a continuing action or indicate the duration of an action. The progressive is formed by combining some form of the verb *to be* with the *ing* form (present participle) of the principal verb.

Verb Tense	Used with	Example
present progressive	actions that are continuing in the present	She **is walking** too fast.
past progressive	actions that were continuing in the past	Cyndi **was eating.**
future progressive	actions that will be continuing in the future	I **will be improving** my diet this school year.
present perfect progressive	action that began in the past and continues into the present	I **have been working** on an exercise plan for the past three weeks.
past perfect progressive	actions in the past that began before a specific time or other action	Before school started, I **had been riding** my bike.
future perfect progressive	continuing actions that will be completed by a specified time in the future	By next month, I **will have been exercising** for one year.

• •

❶ Show What You Know

Underline and label the progressive verb forms in the following letter.

Dear Restaurant Patrons,

More and more diners have been requesting healthy menu choices. It is our pleasure to meet the needs of these health-conscious customers. As you read through our new menu, you will be noticing a variety of new offerings. The restaurant staff has been enjoying the ongoing taste tests of these recent creations. We are hoping that you will enjoy the tofu surprise as much as we do!

Sincerely,

The Tomaine Palace Owners and Staff

Go on

Name _____ Date _____

❷ Take It Up a Notch

Fill in the blanks with the indicated form of the verb in parentheses.

This roving reporter (enter) _____ the first-ever health and fitness fair
present progressive

to be held in our town. As I stroll along, speed walkers (pass) _____
present progressive

me at an impressive rate. Speed walkers (try) _____ to increase the
present perfect progressive

popularity of the activity for decades now. Until the high school team's starting quarterback

developed a serious knee problem from too much running on concrete sidewalks, running and

jogging were very popular here. Quarterback Ricky Wolfe (hope) _____
past perfect progressive

for that coveted football scholarship to State U when his knee trouble sidelined him during

the crucial season. As a result of the injury, Ricky changed his professional direction. In two

years, he (graduate) _____ with a degree in physical therapy.
future progressive

• •

❸ On Your Own

Working with a partner, write a narrative that includes all six of the
progressive forms described in this lesson. When you have completed
a draft of your text, underline each progressive verb form and label it.
This is your master copy. Now produce a copy of your story with blanks
where the progressive forms should be. Use the exercise above as a model.
Then trade stories with another group and fill in the blanks.

Editors' Tips from TIME

✔ Even seasoned writers may have trouble deciding on the correct tense and form of a
verb, but the decision must be made correctly to ensure clear communication with
the audience. Having a clear understanding of the sequence of events that you are
writing about will help you choose the correct verb tense and form. Do what the most
experienced writers sometimes do: check your handbook.

Name _____ Date _____

Irregular Verbs

Verbs that do not form their past tense and past participle forms by following the pattern of most verbs are called **irregular verbs.**

Some Common Irregular Verbs		
Present Stem	**Past Tense**	**Past Participle**
be	was	been
begin	began	begun
choose	chose	chosen
do	did	done
drive	drove	driven
fall	fell	fallen
fly	flew	flown
grow	grew	grown

Some Common Irregular Verbs		
Present Stem	**Past Tense**	**Past Participle**
know	knew	known
lie (to recline)	lay	lain
ride	rode	ridden
speak	spoke	spoken
take	took	taken
throw	threw	thrown
wear	wore	worn
write	wrote	written

❶ Show What You Know

Underline the past tense and past participle forms of irregular verbs in the essay below. The first has been done for you.

Pop artist Andy Warhol <u>said</u> that someday everyone would be famous for 15 minutes. The popularity of reality TV shows has made me think that Warhol was right. It seems that more and more people fantasize about being famous. Some people have achieved fame and found it satisfying, but for others fame has brought them unwanted attention. For instance, many stars are caught off-guard by photographers on the street. They have then found less-than-flattering images of themselves in the tabloids. Even those who have found some happiness in fame often discover that their happiness is short lived. Fame has proven itself, after all, to be fleeting. Perhaps Andy Warhol should have told us that, ultimately, nobody is famous for more than 15 minutes. For a lucky few, those 15 minutes may be happy ones.

Go on

Name _____ Date _____

❷ Take It Up a Notch

Fill in the blanks with the correct form of the irregular verb.

Oprah Winfrey has _____ to fame through her work in television and film as well

rise

as in education and philanthropy. This influential woman _____ her media career

begin

at a radio station in Nashville while still in high school. She was just nineteen years old when

she _____ a news anchor at a Nashville television station. More recently, Winfrey's

become

dynamic personality has _____ her a popular talk show host. Winfrey's generosity

make

has _____ her the gratitude of many, along with worldwide respect. Her Angel

bring

Network has _____ millions of dollars to support scholarships, shelters, youth

give

centers, and other special causes. This charity work _____ her the Bob Hope

win

Humanitarian Award in 2002.

● ● ● ● ● ● ● ● ● ● ● ● ● ● ● ● ● ● ●

❸ On Your Own

Look over the list of irregular verbs identified in this lesson. Choose six
irregular verbs and use them to write a story, report, or essay. Challenge
yourself to stick with the verbs you choose. Let your choices stretch your
imagination and make your readers laugh.

Oprah
Winfrey

Editors' Tips from TIME

✔ Some verbs have two acceptable forms for the past or the past participle form such as
bent/bended and *shined/shone*. It is important to remember that language does change.
Over time, some irregular forms have drifted toward a more regular form. How do you
choose which form to use? Listen to the people around you. What sounds more natural
to you? Often the speakers in a geographic region will favor one form over the other.

Name _____ Date _____

Inverted Order

When the verb comes before the subject in a sentence, the sentence has an **inverted order.**
Confusion about subject-verb agreement can occur when a sentence has an inverted order.
This is a particular problem when there is a compound subject.

$$\overset{\textbf{verb}}{} \quad \overset{\textbf{compound subject}}{}$$

Error: Of concern is the cello and the violin.

Correction: Of concern are the cello and the violin.

Confusion occurs in the above example because the closest noun to the verb is singular. The
writer must recognize that the full subject of the sentence is compound and, therefore, plural.

• •

In sentences that begin with *there is* or *there are*, the verb always precedes the subject.
Be sure to use a plural verb with a compound subject.

$$\overset{\textbf{verb}}{} \quad \overset{\textbf{compound subject}}{}$$

Error: There is a cello and a violin in the repair shop.

Correction: There are a cello and a violin in the repair shop.

• •

Inverted order is used in many interrogative sentences. In interrogative sentences that
begin with *who, what,* and *which,* the subject comes before the verb. This is not true for
interrogative sentences that begin with *whom.* Turn the question into a statement by
reversing the order to find the subject of the sentence.

auxiliary verb subject verb   **subject verb**

Question: Whom did you ask for help?   **Statement:** You asked whom for help.

• •

❶ Show What You Know

**Label the subjects and the verbs in the following inverted-order sentences.
Label main verbs with *v* and auxiliary verbs with *av*. Label subjects with *s*.**

Never will I understand that piece of music.

Indispensable to the violin section is the concertmaster.

Have you ever considered a musical career?

There are the conductor's score and her baton.

When the music stopped, up rose the audience to its feet.

Go on

Name _____   Date _____

❷ Take It Up a Notch

The sentences below are written using the standard subject-verb order. Rewrite them using inverted order. Statements may be turned into questions.

A good ear is important to any musician.

_____

A professional musician must practice regularly.

_____

The repetition of finger exercises will improve dexterity.

_____

The study of scales is essential to musical training.

_____

Proofreading Power!

Using the proofreader's marks in the box, correct the seven errors in the music review below.

This critic feels privileged to have been present for the Civic Orchestra's performance of Beethoven's Ninth Symphony. Of course, I has heard that monumental work many times, but Saturday night's performance was extraordinary. Never I have heard the Ninth played and sung with such passion. As I write this, I am hear that glorious last movement in my heart. From the opening note, I have been pleasantly surprised, even stunned. The new conductor drawed from the orchestra a richness of sound that filled the hall. It is obvious that the singers in the chorus have been preparing for weeks before the concert.

⁋	Indent paragraph
∧	Add
⊙	Add a period
ϑ	Delete
≡	Capitalize
/	Make lowercase
∩∪	Reverse

Name _____ Date _____

Adjectives

Adjectives modify by describing, quantifying, or otherwise limiting the meaning of nouns and pronouns. An adjective tells *what kind* of thing a noun is or *how many* of that thing there are.

> *what kind:*   The **large** seagull landed with surprising grace.
>
> *how many:*   **Three** surfers brave the cold waters of the outer Cape.

• •

Do not use a comma after an adjective that tells how many.

> **Two fat and feisty** gulls fought over a french fry.

• •

Use a hyphen to join two or more words that function as a single adjective before a noun.

> She bent to examine the **pinkish-tan** shell at her feet.
>
> Her **seventy-year-old** grandmother swims in the ocean every day.

• •

❶ Show What You Know

Underline each adjective and circle the modified word or group of words.

My ancestors moved to Cape Cod, a narrow strip of land in Massachusetts, many years ago. Hardly has there been a day when I have not gazed at the changeable waters of the Atlantic. Now that I am leaving for college, I can see that growing up by the deep and mysterious ocean has shaped me. I do not, for instance, take my delicious fish-and-chips for granted because I have watched the exhausted fishermen dock their weather-beaten boats at the end of an arduous trip. While others complain about rough weather, I appreciate it, knowing that it may teach me more than a hundred sunny days on the beach ever will. I have embraced the exhilarating possibilities and the daunting challenges of life in this unique place.

Go on ➡

Name _____   Date _____

❷ Take It Up a Notch

Complete this description of a beach on a summer day by filling in each blank with one or more adjectives. Use your imagination!

The beaches of Cape Cod draw thousands of _____ visitors. I can think of no

place I'd rather be on a(n) _____ summer day. On a(n) _____

and _____ morning, I see dozens of _____ families.

_____ _____ children play at the water's edge while

_____ parents snack on _____ food and watch the

_____ waves. Looking out toward the _____ horizon,

I see _____ _____ _____ ships

and wonder if the people on board can see all the _____ bathers.

As the _____ sun sets behind the _____ dunes, the

_____ beachgoers gather their _____ belongings and

head for home, perhaps for a(n) _____ Cape Cod clambake.

❸ On Your Own

Working with a partner, decide on a place that would make a good subject for a descriptive paragraph. Then, each of you should write your own paragraph, using at least six adjectives to describe the place you both chose. Read your description and listen to your partner's description. Did you include the same details? Did you use the same adjectives?

Editors' Tips from TIME

✔ Adjectives add important details to our writing, making it more lively and interesting for the reader. Nevertheless, beware of using too many adjectives or of using the same adjectives over and over. Keep your descriptions fresh by expanding your vocabulary of adjectives.

Name _____ Date _____

Articles and Demonstrative Adjectives

The words *a*, *an*, and *the* form a special class of adjectives called **articles.** *A* and *an* are called indefinite articles because they refer to any person, place, thing, or idea. *The* is a definite article, referring to a particular person, place, thing, or idea.

• •

Use *a* before words beginning with a consonant sound. Use *an* before words that begin with a vowel sound. The articles *a* and *an* are used only with singular nouns. The definite article is used before both singular and plural nouns.

    a battle   **an** army   **the** generals   **the** history

• •

This, that, these, and *those* are called **demonstrative adjectives** when they appear before a noun. Demonstrative adjectives tell *which one. This* and *these* point out people, places, things, or ideas that are close to the speaker in either time or space. *That* and *those* point out people, places, things, or ideas that are farther away from the speaker. Use *this* and *that* with singular nouns and *these* and *those* with plural nouns.

    close by: **This** message is for you.   **These** boots are worn out.

    farther away: **That** coffee is cold.   **Those** cots were uncomfortable.

• •

❶ Show What You Know

Circle the correct articles and demonstrative adjectives below.

I read a/an extensive history of the/a First World War for my report.

Before I started my research, I did not know that, until the outbreak of

World War II, this/that war was known as the Great War. I also did not

realize that America did not enter that/this war until it was almost over.

The/A people of Britain suffered much more than we did in that/this war

because they were involved from the/a beginning. Many young men

from all a/the countries involved died. Those/These soldiers who returned

were often horribly wounded, both physically and psychologically.

Name _____ Date _____

❷ Take It Up a Notch

**Fill in each blank in the report below with the
correct article or demonstrative adjective.**

Historians generally agree that the international tensions leading to World War I had

been growing for some time before _____ actual start of the war. It was in
                                        article

_____ Balkan country of Serbia, finally, where _____ particular
    article   *article*

incident that led to _____ outbreak of _____ war occurred on June 28,
                          article   *article*

1914. _____ morning, in a street in Sarajevo, _____ bustling capital of
        dem. adj.   *article*

Serbia, Archduke Franz Ferdinand of Austria was assassinated by _____ member
                                                                      article

of a Serbian nationalist movement known as _____ "Black Hand." Exactly one
                                                  article

month later, on July 28, 1914, Austria-Hungary declared war on Serbia. _____
                                                                            article

world would be shocked by _____ brutal battles, now so famous, that continued
                               dem. adj.

until _____ final shots were fired on November 11, 1918.
          article

• •

❸ On Your Own

The article *the* is the most commonly used word in the English language. Do an informal
linguistic research project of your own by tallying the number of articles and demonstrative
adjectives contained on a random page of text from one of your textbooks. Then calculate
what percentage of them are articles and what percentage are demonstrative adjectives.
Which article occurred the most frequently? Which demonstrative adjective was used the most?

Editors' Tips from TIME

✔ When should you use *a* or *an*? Sometimes the answer is not obvious. You will find
it helpful to remember that the choice depends not on spelling, but on sound. For
instance, the word *hour* has a consonant as its first letter, but its first sound is a vowel
sound; therefore, the correct choice of indefinite article is *an*.

Name _____ Date _____

Proper Adjectives

A **proper adjective** is one that is formed from a proper noun. In general, proper adjectives, like proper nouns, are capitalized.

proper noun

My ancestors came from **Poland.**

proper adjective

I'd like to learn about my **Polish** ancestors.

Paul Simon gave a concert in **Zimbabwe.** I like **Zimbabwean** popular music.

• •

A proper adjective is formed from a proper noun by making a spelling change and adding one of these endings: *–an, –ish,* or *–ese.* However, there are exceptions to these guidelines. For instance, the proper adjective *Dutch,* which describes the people who live in Holland and the Netherlands, seems unrelated to either word. There are also proper nouns that do not change form when they are used as proper adjectives, such as *Boston Cream Pie.* Consult a dictionary when you are uncertain about how to turn a proper noun into a proper adjective.

• •

❶ Show What You Know

Fill in the blank in each sentence with the proper adjective formed from the indicated proper noun. If you are uncertain of the spelling, consult a dictionary.

My uncle's _____ cat has a sweet disposition, but terrible breath. His terrible
             Persia

breath probably comes from the _____ herring that my Uncle Ormsbey feeds
                            Finland

him. Uncle Ormsbey started feeding the cat herring after the vet persuaded him that

_____ pastry isn't good for cats, even in moderation. Uncle Ormsbey explains
     France

that his cat, whose name is Alex, is no ordinary cat. For instance, Alex will only take his

catnaps on one of my uncle's _____ shirts. He also likes watching the
                          Hawaii

_____ soccer teams on television with Uncle Ormsbey. Alex's best friend
   Brazil

is Greta. Greta is a _____ shepherd. She sleeps with her head on Uncle
              Germany

Ormsbey's _____ sweater. Meanwhile, Uncle Ormsbey grins as he snacks
       Ireland

on _____ taffy and watches his animal companions dream.
   Turkey

Go on

Name _____ Date _____

❷ Take It Up a Notch

Rewrite the underlined phrase by replacing it with a proper adjective that modifies the noun. Use a dictionary if you are unsure of the proper modification. Here's an example:

> Mitchell enjoys eating <u>licorice from Holland</u>. _____

The <u>culture of the city of Milan</u> is quite old. _____

Mimi learned to play the <u>dulcimer from Appalachia</u>. _____

I often don't understand <u>films made in Sweden</u>. _____

A restaurant serving <u>food from Korea</u> opened in my neighborhood. _____

The <u>economy of Europe</u> is changing. _____

The Statue of Liberty is a famous <u>landmark of New York</u>. _____

This museum has a remarkable collection of <u>artifacts from Egypt</u>. _____

• •

❸ On Your Own

Brainstorm in a small group to make a list of as many countries and continents as you can think of. (Look at a world map or globe if you need to jog your memory.) Do you know the adjectival form of every proper noun on your list? See how many you are sure of, and then check the dictionary for the rest.

Editors' Tips from TIME

✔ As the above exercise demonstrates, a proper adjective can be used in place of a phrase containing a proper noun. Replacing a phrase with a word will help you tighten up your writing. Of course, you may want to keep the phrase for variety or for a particular shade of meaning.

Name _____ Date _____

Predicate Adjectives

When an adjective follows a linking verb, it modifies the subject of the sentence and is called a **predicate adjective** (sometimes called a "subject complement"). The linking verb connects the noun and the adjective that describes or limits it.

predicate adjective \
The recording industry is competitive.

predicate adjective \
The vocal track sounds good.

predicate adjective \
That young artist will become famous.

predicate adjective \
The singer seems confident.

Notice that none of these sentences would be complete without the predicate adjective.

Some Common Linking Verbs				
appear	be	become	feel	remain
taste	smell	seem	sound	look

• •

Some verbs that function as linking verbs can also function in other contexts as action verbs. Consider the difference between the two examples below.

linking verb   predicate adjective \
The engineer looks happy.

action verb   adverb \
The drummer looks happily at the guitarist.

• •

❶ Show What You Know

Label the linking verbs *lv* and the predicate adjectives *pa* below.

That song sounds familiar to me.

That bass part seems difficult.

I am pleased with the band's progress.

With practice, Isabel will become better on the drums.

She feels discouraged.

The lighting is dim, but the acoustics are good.

Fame is unlikely, but the band remains optimistic.

Go on →

Name _____ Date _____

❷ Take It Up a Notch

Label the linking verbs *lv* and the predicate adjectives *pa* in the letter below.

Dear Rock and Roll Hall of Fame Staff:

I am writing to express my appreciation for your help with my research on the history of rock. My visit to Cleveland and the Hall of Fame was rewarding. I am grateful to your staff for introducing me to the accomplishments of William "Smokey" Robinson. Although I had heard of Smokey Robinson and the Miracles, I was unfamiliar with their recordings. I now feel connected to Robinson's voice and his songwriting. No matter what he sings, his voice sounds clear and beautiful. Learning more about his work as a record producer will be interesting. The tour guide was knowledgeable and patient. She was entertaining, too! I especially enjoyed her imitation of Elvis. The exhibits were quite crowded. I looked at the Les Paul guitar exhibit and would certainly like to return and spend more time learning about those amazing instruments. Again, I remain grateful for your help and expertise.

Sincerely,

David Kowalski

Smokey
Robinson

❸ On Your Own

Write a letter of appreciation to someone who has helped you with your education. After you have completed a draft of your letter, underline all the linking verbs and predicate adjectives. Then try to include two more sentences that contain some linking verbs and predicate adjectives that you have not used already.

Editors' Tips from TIME

✔ *Sam feels bad* or *Sam feels badly?* Which is correct? Although saying *badly* is becoming more acceptable in casual speech, *bad* is the better choice when you are writing. The verb *feel* is functioning as a linking verb in the sentence; therefore, it should be followed by a predicate adjective and not by an adverb such as *badly*. Unless you are writing dialogue or quoting someone, it is better to use proper grammar when you write.

Name _____ Date _____

Comparing with Adjectives

To compare two persons, places, things, or ideas, use the **comparative** form of the adjective. To compare three or more, use the **superlative** form of the adjective.

Adjective: The **helpful** librarian showed me a copy of our town's history.

Comparative: The newspaper archives were **more helpful** to me than the library.

Superlative: Great-aunt Elizabeth was the **most helpful** of my elderly relatives.

Forming Comparatives and Superlatives	Adjective	Comparative	Superlative
Most one–syllable adjectives	long	long**er**	long**est**
Adjectives ending in –e	large	larg**er**	larg**est**
Adjectives ending in a consonant and –y	early	earl**ier**	earl**iest**
Adjectives ending in a single vowel and a consonant	red	red**der**	red**dest**
Most adjectives of two or more syllables	vicious	**more** vicious	**most** vicious

Some adjectives that can be changed by adding an ending may also be changed with *more* or *most*. Never use the comparative or superlative ending in addition to *more* or *most*.

• •

Some adjectives are irregular and have unique forms.

Adjective	Comparative	Superlative
good	better	best
bad	worse	worst

Adjective	Comparative	Superlative
much	more	most
little	less	least

• •

❶ Show What You Know

**Underline the comparative and superlative adjectives below.
Label the comparative forms with c and the superlative forms with s.**

To me, true stories are more interesting than fiction. The most interesting stories are those about my ancestors. According to many experts, interviewing the oldest members of your family is one of the most important things you can do. I sat down with Great-uncle Paul, the eldest of my grandfather's three brothers. He told me stories about all the jobs he'd ever had. Each new story he told me was more fascinating than the last.

 Go on

Name _____ Date _____

❷ Take It Up a Notch

Fill in the blanks below with the correct form of the adjective.

Here is a story that my great-aunt Lois told me: "When I graduated from high school in 1940,

I wanted to go to college, but that would have cost _____ money than my family

much

had, so I went to work. I worked in the _____ dress shop in three towns. It was

fancy

on Liberty Street, the _____ street in our _____ town. For months,

busy   small

I stood behind the cash register while girls _____ than I helped the customers.

experienced

Then one day our _____ customer of all asked my opinion of the dress she

elegant

was trying on. I was _____ , telling her that I felt a dress I had seen in another

honest

shop's window would be _____ to her figure. From then on, that elegant lady

flattering

demanded that only I assist her in the shop."

✔ Proofreading Power!

**Read the following introduction to a family history project.
Use proofreader's marks to correct the eight errors below.**

When I began these longer project, I knew little about my families

history. In the process of climbing the branches on the family tree,

I have met second cousins and even my mostest distant relatives.

Everyone has been helpful, but the more helpful of all has been

my great-uncle Paul. He told me the Hungary town from which

my great-great-grandparents emigrated. (You will see an old

photograph of this town in that report.) I would like to dedicate

these report to them.

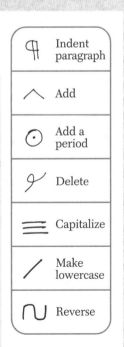

¶	Indent paragraph
⌄	Add
⊙	Add a period
⸮	Delete
≡	Capitalize
/	Make lowercase
∿	Reverse

©TIME Inc.

Name _____ Date _____

Adverbs

An **adverb** is a word that modifies a verb, an adjective, or another adverb. When an adverb modifies a verb, it tells *how, when, where,* or *to what extent.* Most adverbs are formed by adding *–ly* or *–ally* to an adjective. Adverbs such as *here, just,* and *there* do not have endings.

                                                     verb   adverb

How: The conductor motions **impatiently.**

                                verb   adverb

To what extent: Janice sings **quietly.**

Place the adverb as close as possible to the word it modifies. When there is an auxiliary verb and a main verb, the adverb is usually placed between the two. If the verb phrase contains more than one auxiliary verb, place the adverb next to the main verb (*need*).

Awkward: The pit orchestra **probably** <u>will need</u> an extra rehearsal.

Improved: The pit orchestra <u>will **probably** need</u> an extra rehearsal.

When an adverb applies to the entire sentence or when it is used with special emphasis, use it to introduce the sentence.

Happily, I can tell you that we have sold all the tickets.

Place the adverb after the main part of an infinitive verb.

Error: Mark begins <u>to **casually** stroll</u> across the stage.

Correction: Mark begins <u>to stroll **casually**</u> across the stage.

❶ Show What You Know

Circle the adverbs below and underline the words they modify.

At the beginning of the 20th century, European immigrants brought operettas to the American stage. Generally, these highly sentimental works do not appeal to audiences as much today as they did then. But the musical comedy form, with its spoken dialogue, extremely tuneful score, and lavishly furnished stage sets, is not very different from its old-fashioned ancestor, the operetta.

Go on

Name _____   Date _____

❷ Take It Up a Notch

Use an arrow to indicate the best place in the sentence for the adverb in parentheses.

It is opening night. (finally)

Mr. Moses whispers some directions to the leading man. (quietly)

The dancers are learning last-minute changes to their routine. (quickly)

There are five minutes left before the curtain goes up. (only)

Leslie has been working on her makeup for an hour. (intently)

Gail makes a last-minute check of the props for the first act. (hurriedly)

David needs to repair a rip in Cyndi's costume. (speedily)

The musicians have been warming up in the pit. (noisily)

The conductor raises his baton. (silently)

The stagehands begin to pull on the ropes that raise the curtain. (hard)

❸ On Your Own

Write a silly script for your own musical comedy. Include stage directions that provide adverbs for the actors. Be sure to use full sentences for your stage directions and carefully place the adverbs.

Editors' Tips from TIME

✔ In casual speech, *very* and *really* are used frequently as intensifying adverbs. When it comes to formal writing, however, such language is distracting. *Very* and *really* can almost always be edited out without any loss to the power of your wording. (An exception to this rule would be if you were writing a fictional dialogue between two people who use *very* and *really* a lot!) Unless you are deliberately using *very* and *really* to capture the flavor of casual speech, try to find a better way to convey your meaning without relying on such words. Perhaps you can think of a stronger verb or maybe reword the sentence to increase the intensity of your point.

Name _____ Date _____

Comparative Adverbs

To form the **comparative** form of adverbs ending in *–ly*, use the adverb *more*.
To form the **superlative** form of those adverbs, use the adverb *most*.

Positive: Gavin **earnestly** pleaded his case.

Comparative: Sheila pleaded **more earnestly** than Gavin.

Superlative: Amy pleaded **most earnestly** for a change in policy.

● ●

A small number of adverbs take the same endings as adjectives to form the comparative and superlative forms.

Positive: Those students worked **hard.**

Comparative: This class works **harder.**

Superlative: The seniors worked the **hardest** on the project.

● ●

Some adverbs are irregular, having completely different words for their comparative and superlative forms.

Adverb	Comparative	Superlative
well	better	best
badly	worse	worst
little	less	least
much	more	most

● ●

❶ Show What You Know

Underline the adverbs in the following sentences.
Label comparatives with a c and superlatives with an s.

False rumors spread more quickly than the truth.

An information session was most hastily planned.

Shantel distributed flyers faster than we could print them.

Principal Oliver shuffled his papers more noisily than usual.

Denise most carefully arranges the chairs in rows.

Go on

Name _____ Date _____

❷ Take It Up a Notch

Fill in each blank with the correct adverbial form of the word in parentheses.
Label each adverb with either *p* for positive, *c* for comparative, or *s* for superlative.

Until _____ (recent), I attended a school that required uniforms. In my top

dresser drawer, I had _____ (neat) arranged five pairs of white socks for gym class.

Next to those gym socks, I had even _____ (neat) arranged five pairs of navy blue

socks. Hanging in my closet were five white shirts that I had _____ (expert) ironed.

Next to those shirts hung the tie that I treasured _____ (dear) of all, the tie

my little sister made for me. That tie sports the _____ (meticulous) painted

portrait of a gopher.

Proofreading Power!

Correct the ten errors in the following letter.
Use the proofreader's marks from the box.

Dear Principal Oliver:

     I most recent heard about the adoption of school uniforms

for all currently students. You probably are thinking that I want to

passionately plead against the adoption of a uniform policy. I say

respectfullies that you are wrong about my position. You could

not be surpriseder than I am by my stand on this issue, but I have

thought hardly about the pros and cons of uniforms. If you would

like to discuss this issue with me, I would be happy to discuss

honestly it with you.

               Sincere,
               I.M. Natty

⁋	Indent paragraph
⌃	Add
⊙	Add a period
⌿	Delete
☰	Capitalize
/	Make lowercase
∩	Reverse

Name _____ Date _____

Negatives

A **negative** is a modifying word that means "no." Using a negative changes the meaning of a sentence. Often, there is more than one way to change a positive statement into a negative statement.

Positive: The players are in the gym.

Negative: The players are **not** in the gym.

Negative: The players **aren't** in the gym.

Some Common Negatives			
no	not	none	no one
nothing	never	nowhere	nobody
aren't	can't	couldn't	doesn't
haven't	isn't	wouldn't	won't

• •

Do not use two negatives in the same clause of a sentence. This error is called a "double negative."

Incorrect: She **hasn't never** played volleyball on the beach.

Correct: She has **never** played volleyball on the beach.

Correct: She **hasn't** played volleyball on the beach.

• •

❶ Show What You Know
Underline the negatives in the report below.

According to the *Federation Internationale de Volleyball* (FIVB), the first official rules

for volleyball were not written down until the 1890s. The rules were invented in

Holyoke, Massachusetts, by William G. Morgan, a YMCA physical education director.

At first he did not call it volleyball; he called the game "Mintonette." It wasn't until

a demonstration game of Mintonette was played at the YMCA in Springfield,

Massachusetts, that the name of the game was changed. Today nobody plays

"Mintonette," but many people play "volleyball."

Go on

Name _____ Date _____

❷ Take It Up a Notch

Rewrite each sentence below, correcting the double negative.

There aren't no volleyball players in my homeroom this year.

_____

My cousin's school hasn't never had a volleyball team.

_____

Our volleyball team won't never lose.

_____

I'm not no good at serving the ball.

_____

✔ Proofreading Power!

**Correct the six errors in the following letter to a newspaper.
Use the proofreader's marks from the box.**

Dear Sports Editor:

    I am writing to ask that you begin covering the volleyball games in our area. I can't hardly believe it, but some people haven't never seen a volleyball game played by a team of trained athletes. You might not see no problem in this, but think about how volleyball could change people's lives. It would not take no great effort on your part to bring volleyball to more people's attention. Don't you have no interest in our sport? Isn't there never some player you'd like to write about?

                Sincerely,

                Joyce Woijek

¶	Indent paragraph
⌃	Add
⊙	Add a period
✄	Delete
≡	Capitalize
/	Make lowercase
∩	Reverse

©TIME Inc.

Name _____ Date _____

Prepositions and Prepositional Phrases

A **preposition** shows the relationship of a noun, a pronoun, or a phrase to another word in the sentence. The noun or pronoun that follows the preposition is called the **object of the preposition.** The preposition, its object, and any adjectives that modify the object form a **prepositional phrase.**

preposition   adjective   object of the preposition

Shirley hangs wallpaper [in the smallest bedroom.]

prepositional phrase

• •

These are some of the most common prepositions.

Prepositions				
about	behind	except	near	since
above	below	for	of	through
after	between	from	on	to
among	by	in	out	toward
around	down	inside	over	up
before	during	into	past	with

• •

While most prepositions are one word, **phrasal prepositions** are made up of two or more words. They should be treated as a single unit.

phrasal preposition

Because of water damage, we must replace this ceiling.

prepositional phrase

• •

If the object of the preposition is a pronoun, then that pronoun must be made into an object pronoun.

    Incorrect: Justin framed the painting for **she.**

    Correct: Justin framed the painting for **her.**

• •

When you speak about two persons or things, use the preposition *between.*
When you speak about three or more people or things, use the preposition *among.*

    The tasks were divided **among** Gus, Mandy, and Arnie.

Go on

Name _____ Date _____

❶ Show What You Know

Circle the prepositions and underline the prepositional phrases in the paragraph below.

Shirley and Michael are redecorating their house. In the living room, you'll see three shades of green paint. The couple is deciding among those three shades. Michael is leaning toward the darkest shade, but Shirley likes the lightest one.

• •

❷ Take It Up a Notch

Fill in the missing prepositions in this advertisement for a kitchen stove.

Are you still cooking _____ a wood stove? Probably not. But isn't it time

_____ an update _____ that old gas or electric stove? Admit it. The

temperature _____ your oven has never been even. You have burned too many

cookies—_____ no fault _____ your own! Our new stove, the Mega

Chef Supreme, will never disappoint you. _____ the clear oven door, you can

watch your batch of cookies slowly brown or your favorite casserole bubble. The top

_____ your new stove will astound you! The burners are built _____

a flat and smooth surface. No longer will you have to tolerate crevices holding globs

_____ grease and gobs _____ grime! Aren't you ready to enjoy

cooking meals _____ family and friends again?

• • • • • • • • • • • • • • • • • •

❸ On Your Own

Write an advertisement for a household appliance of your own invention. Using as many different prepositions as you can, describe in great detail what your invention is and what it does. Exchange advertisements with a classmate and see if you can draw an illustration for his or her advertisement.

Name _____ Date _____

Adjective Phrases and Adverb Phrases

As you know, a preposition, its object, and any of its modifiers form a prepositional phrase. When a prepositional phrase modifies a noun or a pronoun, it is called an **adjective phrase.** An **adjective phrase** answers the question *what kind* or *which one.* A prepositional phrase that modifies a verb, adjective, or adverb is called an **adverb phrase.** An adverb phrase answers the question *where, when,* or *how.*

                                                   preposition   adjective   object of preposition

Adjective phrase: Tim is reading a book about volcanic eruptions.

                                         preposition   object of preposition

Adverb phrase: Mount St. Helens is located in Washington State.

To avoid unnecessary awkwardness or confusion, both adjective phrases and adverb phrases should be as close to the word or words they modify as the patterns of idiomatic English will allow.

Confusing: Tim asked the instructor **with a concerned look** when the volcano might erupt.

Awkward: Tim asked **with a concerned look** the instructor when the volcano might erupt.

Improved: **With a concerned look,** Tim asked the instructor when the volcano might erupt.

❶ Show What You Know

Label each underlined prepositional phrase in the sentences below as either an adjective phrase (*adj*) or an adverb phrase (*adv*).

The ancient volcano Krakatoa is located <u>in a highly active volcanic area</u>.

The eruption <u>of Krakatoa</u> <u>in August 1883</u> was massive.

The sound <u>of the eruption</u> traveled more than 2,000 miles.

<u>For more than two days</u>, clouds <u>of volcanic ash</u> shut out the light.

Dust <u>from the explosion</u> encircled the earth, creating sunsets <u>of brilliant color</u>.

Name _____   Date _____

❷ Take It Up a Notch

Revise the sentences below by moving the misplaced prepositional phrase.

In history, the most devastating tsunami took place on December 25, 2004.

_____

That tsunami was by an underwater earthquake caused.

_____

By countries at risk, tsunami warning systems must be developed.

_____

Proofreading Power!

Using the proofreader's marks in the box, correct the five errors in the letter below.

Dear Tim:

    Thank you for writing to me at the university's geology department. Certainly, you must take physical science courses. Completing the prerequisite courses in science and math for advanced physics will give you for beginning your studies here at the university a solid background. Don't neglect the life sciences. You should take advanced biology and any specialized courses that your school offers. If your school offers a course in botany, you should take it for instance because the study of how an area's plant and animal life recovers from a major geologic event is important. With your studies, I wish you luck.

                    Sincerely,
                    Professor Jamie Rothrock, Ph.D.

¶	Indent paragraph
∧	Add
⊙	Add a period
ℛ	Delete
≡	Capitalize
/	Make lowercase
∿	Reverse

Name _____ Date _____

Subject and Object Pronouns

A pronoun always refers to a noun called the antecedent. Antecedents usually appear in the same sentence as the pronoun but may show up in a nearby sentence. Two types of pronouns are **subject** and **object pronouns.**

Subject Pronouns	I	you	he	she	it	we	you	they	who
Object Pronouns	me	you	him	her	it	us	you	them	whom

• •

Use a subject pronoun when the pronoun is the subject of the sentence or if it is a subject complement following a form of the verb *to be.* Use an object pronoun when the pronoun is the object of an action verb or the object of a preposition. This rule applies to compound subjects as well as single subjects.

                            antecedent   subject pronoun   subject pronoun

Subject pronouns: There is Aunt Marion. **Who** owns the farm? **She** does.

                       object pronoun   antecedent   subject pronoun

Object pronouns: For **whom** did Aunt Marion make this dinner? **It** is for us.

• •

❶ Show What You Know

Underline the subject and object pronouns in the personal essay below. Double-underline the compound subjects and objects that contain a subject or object pronoun. Label subject pronouns with *sub.* and object pronouns with *obj.*

Visiting my Aunt Marion and Uncle Tom at Hillside Farm makes me question the way we live our lives. My family and I seem to rush from one thing to the next. Consider my sister, Louise. She has a piano lesson on Monday after school. On Tuesday, she and I go together to basketball practice. On Wednesday, it is an Explorers Club meeting. Thursday, it is tutoring, and on Friday, dancing. I admit that Louise enjoys all she does, but when she and I visit our aunt and uncle, I wonder if we aren't missing something. For them, life is slower. Yet they never complain about being bored. Maybe Mom, Dad, Louise, and I need to learn from them and have more quiet time in our lives.

Go on

Name _____ Date _____

❷ Take It Up a Notch

Circle the correct subject or object pronoun in the journal entry below.

We/Us arrived at the farm just as it began to snow. The flakes looked beautiful in the moonlight.

They/Them fell silently, and Carrie and I/me jumped when we/us heard an owl hoot. Adjusting

to the quiet of the farm can be difficult for I/me. My everyday life is so busy and noisy that the

quiet here can make I/me nervous. My dad loves to come here because this is where he/him

grew up. For my mother and he/him, this is a time to get away, they/them say, from all the noise

of living with teenagers. My aunt and uncle like quiet, too. It is unusual for they/them to have

the television on. Hmm. I/me wonder if Mom, Dad, Carrie, and I/me could get used to this.

❸ On Your Own

Make up your own example sentences about a family trip, real or imagined, and use every
subject and every object pronoun listed in this lesson at least once. Be sure to include at
least three compound subjects and three compound objects that use pronouns.

Editors' Tips from TIME

✔ When you are uncertain about using a subject or an object pronoun in a compound
structure, try simplifying the sentence to see which sounds right. Consider the proper
pronoun for this sentence: "Pass the maple syrup to Carrie and (I/me)." You might be
tempted to choose the subject pronoun *I*, but if you simplify the sentence, you'll hear
that "Pass the maple syrup to I." is wrong. *Me*, the object pronoun, sounds more natural.

Name _____ Date _____

Possessive Pronouns

A **possessive pronoun** shows ownership and takes the place of a possessive noun.

Kathleen's strongest interest is Russian history. **Her** reading list is extensive.

Whereas some possessive pronouns have to be followed by a noun, others can be used alone.

Requiring a following noun: **Their** library has many volumes on Russian history.

Capable of standing alone: **Ours** has a smaller collection on the subject.

Possessive Pronouns			
Used Before Nouns		**Used Alone**	
Singular	**Plural**	**Singular**	**Plural**
my	our	mine	ours
your	your	yours	yours
his, her, its	their	his, hers, its	theirs

Czar Nicholas II and family

Note that while we make a noun possessive by using an apostrophe, this is never the case with possessive pronouns.

Incorrect: The credit is your's.   **Correct:** The credit is yours.

❶ Show What You Know

Circle the correct possessive pronouns in the report below.

Czar Nicholas II and his wife, the Czarina Alexandra, had five children. (Their/Theirs) first

four children were daughters. Nicholas and Alexandra were anxious for a son. Russian law

said that only a son could inherit the throne of (his/his') father. Finally, the couple succeeded

in having a son. (His/His's) name was Alexis. Sadly, the boy was born with a rare inherited

blood disease called hemophilia. Alexandra was particularly sad because she knew that it

was (her/hers) family that carried the disease. Although Alexandra was hit particularly hard,

the entire Romanov family suffered due to Alexis's affliction. There is no happy

ending to the story of the Romanovs. (Their/Theirs) was a tragic story.

Go on ➡

Name _____ Date _____

❷ Take It Up a Notch

Fill in the blanks with the correct possessive pronoun.

In 1917, Russia had a revolution. The Czar was forced to give up _____ throne.

Nicholas, Alexandra, and _____ children were forced to leave _____ palace.

Alexandra was most concerned about the health of _____ son, Alexis. All parents

can experience difficulty protecting _____ children from harm, but Alexis's

hemophilia made Nicholas and Alexandra's task especially stressful. Hemophilia is incurable

and _____ symptoms can be both painful and fatal. If Alexis suffered a cut,

_____ blood would not clot properly to stop the bleeding. To help protect him,

a sailor was assigned to watch over _____ every move. Even following the Romanovs'

capture and imprisonment, Alexis was allowed the protection of _____ sailor.

Alas, a personal guard could not save Alexis and his family from _____ terrible fate.

• •

❸ On Your Own

Alexis's great-grandmother was Queen Victoria of Great Britain. Nicknamed the "Grandmother of Europe" for her close family connection to numerous European rulers, Victoria ruled Great Britain for nearly seven decades. Research the life of this fascinating queen either online or in a library. Take notes while you are researching and then write a summary of your findings. Use as many possessive pronouns as you can.

Queen Victoria

Editors' Tips from TIME

✔ A common error writers make involves the possessive pronoun *its*, which is often confused with *it's*, the contraction of *it is*. It is easy to avoid making this error if you remember that possessive pronouns are not spelled with an apostrophe. Also, do not confuse the possessive pronoun *their* with its homophone *there*.

Name _____   Date _____

Reflexive/Intensive Pronouns

Reflexive and intensive pronouns all end with the suffix *-self* or the suffix *-selves* if plural. A pronoun is reflexive when it refers back to the subject of the verb. In other words, a reflexive pronoun shows that the doer and the receiver of the action are the same. A pronoun is intensive when it is used to emphasize or intensify a noun or another pronoun.

Reflexive: <u>Ella</u> helped **herself** to a copy of the itinerary.

Intensive: <u>I</u> **myself** do not like to fly.

Reflexive/Intensive Pronouns			
myself	yourself	herself	himself
itself	ourselves	yourselves	themselves

• •

Using a reflexive pronoun in place of a personal pronoun in a compound subject is a common error.

Incorrect: Communicating in German was difficult for **Doug and myself**.

Correct: Communicating in German was difficult for **Doug and me**.

• •

❶ Show What You Know

Underline the reflexive and intensive pronouns in the paragraph below. If the pronoun is used as a reflexive pronoun, label it with an *r*. If it is used as an intensive pronoun, label it with an *i*.

Next month Ms. Reed's German students are going to Germany. They are planning the trip themselves. Making the arrangements is educational itself. Doug spoke to the hotel manager in German to confirm the reservations himself. One month from today, Ms. Reed will find herself in Berlin with 25 jet-lagged teenagers. Luckily, Mr. Meier and Ms. Graff will be going on the trip, too. They speak German well themselves and should be a tremendous help. I am looking forward to our first walk on *Unter den Linden,* Berlin's most famous street. I can see myself walking under the linden trees as I write this! Now I must make myself study German before the trip!

Go on ➡

Name _____ Date _____

❷ Take It Up a Notch

Fill in the blank in each sentence with the correct reflexive or intensive pronoun.

Beth volunteered _____ as a student tour assistant.

Help _____ to a free map of Berlin!

The students _____ proposed a trip on the *U-Bahn,* Berlin's subway system.

Ms. Reed ordered a dinner of pork and sauerkraut for _____ .

Mr. Meier treated _____ to *Lebkuchen,* German gingerbread.

"You get _____ to bed early tonight," Ms. Reed told the travelers.

I always go to bed early _____ .

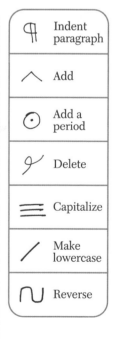

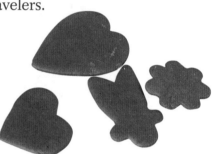

Proofreading Power!

Find and correct the seven errors in the student newspaper article below. Use the proofreader's marks in the box.

Never in the history of our school has a field trip taken students quite so far afield. Ms. Reed's German students found themselfs putting there language skills to good use last month. I mineself was one of those lucky students. Us visited the city of Berlin for several days. Ourselves and our chaperones visited the Kaiser Wilhelm Memorial Church. The church, which suffered major damage in World War II, stands half-ruined and half-renewed. After the war, Berliners decided to remind himself of the destruction all wars cause by letting the ruin stand in the center of there city.

¶	Indent paragraph
∧	Add
⊙	Add a period
⟍	Delete
⹀	Capitalize
/	Make lowercase
∩	Reverse

Name _____   Date _____

Coordinating Conjunctions

A word that connects and shows a relationship between words or groups of words is called a conjunction. **Coordinating conjunctions** are used to join grammatically equal elements, such as words in a series or simple sentences. These conjunctions may indicate added information, contrast, or choice.

Coordinating Conjunctions	and	but	or	nor	for	so	yet

Use *but* or *yet* to show a contrast: I like music, **but** I don't like jazz.

Use *or* to show a choice: Should I study the clarinet **or** the oboe?

Use *so* to show cause and effect: I enjoyed the sound of the clarinet, **so** I decided to take lessons.

• •

The coordinating conjunctions *and* and *or* are frequently used to connect items in a series. Although you may use a conjunction between each element in a series, usually the conjunction is placed before the final item.

Ann can play the trombone, the drums, **and** the violin.

Coordinating conjunctions are also used to join two simple sentences to form a compound sentence. Compound sentences will be covered in more detail in the next lesson.

• •

❶ Show What You Know

Circle the coordinating conjunctions in the paragraph below.

Most classical musicians and music lovers know something about famous European composers. The names Bach, Beethoven, Mozart, and Wagner appear regularly on concert programs, but the names of American composers do not appear nearly as often. I decided to learn about some American composers and listen to their music, so I asked the school librarian for help. He showed me how to use encyclopedias and databases to find information on American music. I learned about the lives of many American composers, yet it was difficult to find recordings of their music in our library.

Go on

Name _____   Date _____

❷ Take It Up a Notch

Insert coordinating conjunctions in the paragraph below.

After doing some preliminary research, I decided to write a report on the early accomplishments of Amy Beach. She was born Amy Marcy Cheney in New Hampshire in 1867, _____ at the extraordinarily early age of four, she began composing music. Amy's parents would have liked her to study abroad, _____ they could not afford to send her, _____ she began studying music in Boston at the age of eight. There she met the poet Henry Wadsworth Longfellow. His poetry inspired her, _____ she composed a song based on his poem "The Rainy Day." It would be her first published song. At the age of sixteen, Amy made her debut as a professional pianist, _____ soon after she was a soloist with the Boston Symphony Orchestra. She continued to compose. Her early works show the influence of Brahms and Wagner. Today's concert programs may list her name as Amy Beach, _____ this was not the case in her own day. After she was married _____ for decades after her death in 1944, she was most often listed as Mrs. H.H.A. Beach. That was how her husband preferred to see her name.

• •

❸ On Your Own

Work with a partner to write the biography of an imaginary composer. Use as many coordinating conjunctions as you can. You might include a list of instruments that the composer wrote for or titles of compositions. Be sure to include at least one coordinating conjunction that shows contrast.

Editors' Tips from TIME

✔ Should you use a conjunction to begin a sentence? In your most formal writing, it is best to avoid beginning a sentence with a conjunction. However, conjunctions may sometimes be used as a way to emphasize an idea or to vary your sentence beginnings.

Name _____ Date _____

Compound and Complex Sentences

A **compound sentence** is made up of at least two independent clauses joined by a comma and a coordinating conjunction. An independent clause is a group of words that includes a subject and a predicate; it could stand alone as a simple sentence.

> **Simple sentence:**   The creek flowed slowly. The woods were silent.
>
> **Compound sentence:**   The creek flowed slowly**, and** the woods were silent.

• •

A **complex sentence** is made up of a main clause, which is an independent clause, and one or more clauses that are subordinate to it. A subordinate clause begins with a subordinating conjunction or a relative pronoun. A complex sentence may begin with either the main clause or the subordinate one.

> **Complex sentence:**   **After** the breakfast bell rang,———— subordinate clause
>   the campers lined up at the dining hall.———— main clause
>
> **Complex sentence:**   The campers lined up at the dining hall —— main clause
>   **after** the breakfast bell rang.———— subordinate clause

If the complex sentence begins with the subordinate clause, that clause must be separated from the main clause by a comma. If the main clause begins the sentence, separate the clauses with a comma only if you want to place special emphasis on the subordinate clause. Beware of mistaking a subordinate clause for a complete sentence.

• •

❶ Show What You Know

Label each sentence as either compound or complex.

As soon as the Nature Girls arrived at Camp Crooked Creek, they began to pitch their

tents. Some campers gathered wood, and others carried water from the camp's well.

After enough firewood had been gathered, a counselor showed the campers how to

build a safe campfire. Because everyone was hungry, the campers began to prepare

their meal. Everyone looked forward to the s'mores they would make after the meal,

and they wanted to sing old camp songs, too. Finally, all the songs had been sung,

and it was time to retire to the tents for a peaceful night in the woods.

Go on

Name _____ Date _____

❷ Take It Up a Notch

Join each pair of clauses to make the kind of sentence named in parentheses.

the creek water may not be safe to drink   we must pack water purification tablets **(complex)**

_____

Kendra bought a new sleeping bag   Jenna bought a new backpack   **(compound)**

_____

we don't want to get wet   we need to pack raingear   **(complex)**

_____

counselors will help us pitch tents   we will learn to mark a trail   **(compound)**

_____

Proofreading Power!

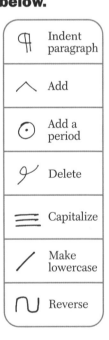

Using the proofreader's marks in the box, correct the six errors below.

Dear Ms. Walters:

I would like to present myself, as a candidate for the counselor-in-training program at Camp Crooked Creek. Since you are the director of that program. I am sending my resume to you. I have never been a camper at Crooked Creek but I have a great deal of camping experience. Even though I have never been a counselor. I have proven my leadership skills as a patrol leader at camp, as a member of the student council at school. I feel that I could serve Camp Crooked Creek well because I will come into the training program with both camping and leadership experience.

Yours truly,
Sunny Days

¶	Indent paragraph
⌃	Add
⊙	Add a period
⤸	Delete
≡	Capitalize
/	Make lowercase
∩∪	Reverse

Name _____ Date _____

Titles of Books, Magazines, Poems, and Songs

Titles of All Works: Capitalize the first word, the last word, and all nouns, pronouns, adjectives, verbs, adverbs, and subordinating conjunctions in any title of a work.

    Poem: "Stopping by Woods on a Snowy Evening"

    Novel: *The Secret of the Old Clock*

• •

Titles of Longer Works: Titles of books, magazines, television shows, movies, and other long works should be either underlined or printed in italics.

Books:	Gulliver's Travels	*Eragon*
Magazines:	*Time*	Fly-Fishing Monthly
Newspapers:	The Jenkinsville Gazette	*The New York Times*
Movies:	Plan 9 from Outer Space	*Swiss Family Robinson*
TV shows:	Masterpiece Theatre	*Andy of Mayberry*

• •

Titles of Shorter Works: The titles of poems, short stories, songs, book chapters, and articles from magazines and newspapers should be enclosed in quotation marks.

Songs:	"I Want to Hold Your Hand"	"Dust Bowl Blues"
Short stories:	"To Build a Fire"	"The Necklace"
Articles:	"How to Organize Your Closet"	"Be an Educated Voter"
Book chapters:	"A Misunderstanding"	"General Grant"

Name _____ Date _____

❶ Show What You Know

Underline the titles of longer works and enclose the titles of shorter works in quotation marks.

poem: The Wasp

short story: Young Goodman Brown

novel: White Fang

song: Lemon Tree

newspaper: The Chicago Tribune

chapter: The Revolution Begins

book: The Life of Ida Tarbell

song: Ebb Tide

article: A Miracle Diet

movie: The Attack of the Blob

Proofreading Power!

Find and correct the errors in the titles of works. There are nine errors.

Welcome to our school library. Here you will find such great old works as the novel "A Tale of two Cities" by Charles Dickens and great contemporary novels such as "A Tale of Cyberspace." You will also find poetry. Here is one of my favorite poems by Edgar Allan Poe. It is titled <u>The Haunted Palace</u>. If you enjoy reading plays, you might want to read this amusing one by Shakespeare: "Twelfth Night." Over here we have newspapers and magazines. You'll find our local paper, "The Daily Disgrace," as well as more important newspapers such as the "Washington Post." The library subscribes to several fine magazines. Here is <u>cricket</u> for the younger kids. And look, here's an article in "Time" on educational standards. Finally, here is our collection of movies. It's not a large collection, but we do have my favorite: "Chitty Chitty Bang Bang."

¶	Indent paragraph
⌃	Add
⊙	Add a period
⟋	Delete
⹀	Capitalize
/	Make lowercase
∾	Reverse

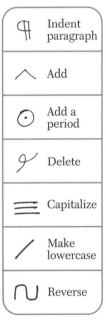

Name _____ Date _____

Commas

A comma used in the right place helps your reader understand what you have written. A comma separates one element of a sentence from another. Typically, a comma signals a slight pause to a person who is reading the text aloud.

• •

Use a comma to set off words of direct address from the rest of the sentence. The word or words of address may come at the beginning of a sentence, in the middle, or at the end. If the address comes in the middle of the sentence, place a comma before and a comma after the address.

Direct address: **Fellow students,** we must work together to make a better school.

Could you, **Ms. Francis,** help us organize a committee?

Please collect the ballots, **Tom.**

• •

Use commas to separate words or groups of words in a series. Place a comma after each word in the series except the last one.

Series: The cafeteria will serve **fish sticks, wax beans, wheat bread, and apples.**

• •

Use a comma before the coordinating conjunctions *and, but,* and *or* when they link independent clauses in a compound sentence.

Compound sentence: Cindy brings plants to the classroom, **and** Mark hangs artwork.

• •

A noun or pronoun placed beside another noun or pronoun to further identify or explain it is called an *appositive.* Set off an appositive from the rest of the sentence with a comma or commas. If the appositive is necessary to identify the noun, it should not be set off with a comma. The punctuation is necessary only when the appositive provides extra information.

Appositive: Mr. Rogers, **my music teacher,** encouraged me to continue.

• •

Nonrestrictive clauses are those that are not essential to the meaning of the main clause of the sentence. Nonrestrictive clauses often begin with *who* or *which* and should be set off by commas. Be careful not to mistake a nonrestrictive clause for a simple sentence.

Nonrestrictive clause: The courtyard, **which is open only to seniors,** is a favorite place for study.

Go on

Name _____   Date _____

❶ Show What You Know

Using the information on the previous page, identify the reason for the comma or commas in each sentence.

We are discussing instituting a dress code, a later starting time, and extended

lunch periods. _____

My classmates are enthusiastic, and they are willing to work hard for their school. _____

Our principal, who graduated from this school, is open to discussing our ideas. _____

Vernon, could you help us write this report? _____

Proofreading Power!

Use the proofreader's marks to correct the 12 comma-related errors in the passage below.

Our class president Kelly called the meeting to order. All the class officers, and 25 class members were in attendance. The president opened the floor for discussion on the extended lunch period and the response from those in attendance was immediate. A number of students were excited about the possibility of a later start to the school day but other students pointed out that a later start might mean a later dismissal. The president suggested that Irwin the class vice president research what has happened at other schools. Sheila, opened a discussion on the extended lunch period and, she suggested that having a longer lunch might lengthen the school day too. She offered to do some research on the issue and the president thanked her.

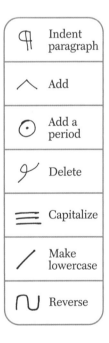

¶	Indent paragraph
∧	Add
⊙	Add a period
℘	Delete
≡	Capitalize
/	Make lowercase
∿	Reverse

Name _____ Date _____

Abbreviations

An **abbreviation** is a shortened form of a word or term that is used often. Use an abbreviation only when you are certain that your readers will easily understand it. Abbreviations are commonly used in addresses. Each state in the United States has an official abbreviation, which is designated by the U.S. Postal Service.

Mr. Matthew Doe
501 Kumquat **St.**
Orono, **ME** 04463

• •

An abbreviation usually begins with a capital letter and ends with a period, but some abbreviations begin with capital letters and do not end with periods, whereas others have neither capital letters nor periods. Study the chart below to familiarize yourself with some of the more common abbreviations.

Common Abbreviations						
state names	NC	North Carolina	PA	Pennsylvania	MO	Missouri
other place names	Ave. Blvd. Apt.	Avenue Boulevard Apartment	St. UK	Street United Kingdom	Mt.	Mount
professional, official, and business titles	Dr. Prof. Sen.	Doctor Professor Senator	RN CEO MD	Registered Nurse Chief Executive Officer Medical Doctor		
measurements	in. oz.	inch ounce	ft. lb.	foot pound	yd. kg	yard kilogram
time	hr. Jan.	hour January	min. a.m.	minute *ante meridiem* (before noon)	mo. Mon.	month Monday
agencies and organizations	UN	United Nations	NPR	National Public Radio		
science and technology	FM RAM	frequency modulation random-access memory			kW	kilowatt

Go on

Name _____ Date _____

❶ Show What You Know

Write the correct abbreviation for each word or term. There may be more than one acceptable answer for some examples. Check a recently published large dictionary for help.

Idaho _____   kilometer _____   Reverend _____

Alabama _____   read-only memory _____   August _____

(your state) _____   Company _____   quart _____

Proofreading Power!

Use the proofreader's marks to correct the 11 problems with abbreviations in the personal letter below.

Dear Poindexter,

    I was glad to hear from you! It was dec when I last heard from you, and I was beginning to think you'd forgotten me. Summer camp seems so long ago, doesn't it? Well, Aug was a long time ago, I guess. Remember when we climbed Mt Cumbersome? I thought we'd never get to the top of that mountain. It must have been a gazillion Ft high! A lot has happened since I last wrote to you. My oldest sister has started her second semester at Ucla. She is working toward her BA in political science. She is still playing a lot of basketball because she wants to try out for the WNbA. someday. My sister likes going to college in ca, but I think I'd like to go to a college in another state—maybe Ak or even hI! Write again soon! I love snail mail!

               Your pal,
               Rachel

¶	Indent paragraph
∧	Add
⊙	Add a period
℘	Delete
≡	Capitalize
/	Make lowercase
∩	Reverse

Name _____ Date _____

Other Punctuation

An **interjection** is a word or expression that indicates feeling. Sometimes an interjection stands alone and sometimes it is part of a sentence. When a strong interjection stands alone, it is followed by an exclamation mark. When a mild interjection is part of a sentence, it is set off by a comma or commas.

> **Congratulations!** You won the contest!

> That was**, well,** a spectacular exhibition.

● ●

A **colon** is a punctuation mark used to introduce or to call attention to what follows and is used in a variety of contexts. It is used for separating elements in a long list, when introducing a quotation after a full sentence, and after the salutation in a formal letter.

> Before leaving, you should have the following items**:** canvas, sketch pad, pencils, erasers, paints, and brushes.

> I have taken Socrates' wisdom to heart**:** "There is only one good, knowledge, and one evil, ignorance."

A colon is also used to separate elements in time, ratios, and titles with subtitles.

> **time:**   The train is due at 6**:**45 this evening.
>
> **ratios:** 2**:**1
>
> **titles:** *Beach Plums with Squid***:** *A Seascape*

● ●

A **semicolon** indicates a pause that is longer than the pause indicated by a comma, but not as long as the full stop that is indicated by a period. Use a semicolon to join two independent clauses not linked by a conjunction and a comma. The semicolon indicates a close relationship between the two clauses.

> The library will be closed for the holiday**;** returns should be made to the drop box.

Semicolons should also be used to separate items in a series when each item contains commas or other punctuation marks.

> In my closet I found a hat**;** a blue, red, and green coat**;** and my fuzzy slippers.

● ●

An **ellipsis mark** is made up of three spaced periods. Use it to indicate an omission within a quoted sentence or statement. Generally, the ellipsis is not needed when an omission occurs at the beginning or end of a quotation.

> Our local art critic said, "These young artists **. . .** enrich our little community."

Go on

Name _____ Date _____

❶ Show What You Know

Fill in the missing exclamation points, ellipsis marks, commas, semicolons, and colons.

Oh, no It's already 3 00 in the afternoon I have to deliver my work to the judges of the art show by 4 00. I know I'll forget something if I don't make a list. Here is what I need to take with me to the gallery my painting a hammer, in case they don't have one extra wire, a long piece and the label I made to attach to the frame. Well I think that's all I'll need. I'm taking the time to write this down because I read the following in a magazine article "Don't trust your memory especially when you are under pressure." Wow Those are words to live by

Proofreading Power!

There are seven punctuation errors in the review below. Correct them using the proofreader's marks.

Last night at exactly 7;00 I walked into our town's high school. I've never seen such a transformation! Vibrant and engaging works of art hang on walls once covered by fading travel posters. These paintings and the drawings are not works by professionals from the big city, they are works by the young people of our own small town. I gazed at portraits of our mayor and our police chief: seascapes of astonishing power and drama; a still life that seemed to move, and landscapes to rival any done by the Hudson River Valley artists. The fact that the art; skill, craft, and dedication necessary to produce these works resides in our small corner of the world makes me proud. As my own high school art teacher once said; "Art should , , , make you wonder, not make you sure."

⁋	Indent paragraph
⌃	Add
⊙	Add a period
⸜	Delete
≡	Capitalize
/	Make lowercase
∩	Reverse

©TIME Inc.

Name _____   Date _____

Quotations and Dialogue

There are some general rules that must be followed when quoting another source. You must enclose a speaker's exact words within quotation marks, capitalizing the first word of the quotation if it is a full sentence. If the quoted material is introduced by a signal phrase, a comma is necessary to separate the quoted words from the rest of the sentence. The signal phrase may be placed before, after, or in the middle of the quoted material. If the quoted material is integrated into the structure of the sentence, neither a comma nor an initial capital letter should be used. As a general rule, place punctuation marks inside the quotation marks, unless it is an exclamation point or question mark that refers to the whole sentence and not just the quotation.

signal phrase

The Greek writer Homer said, "A companion's words of persuasion are effective."

signal phrase

In Shakespeare's play, the character Hamlet says, "To be, or not to be, that is the question."

integrates quoted material

When he was in prison, Nelson Mandela said that "prisoners cannot enter into contracts."

refers to whole sentence

Did you recognize Hamlet's speech, "To be, or not to be, that is the question"?

• •

When you write **dialogue,** a conversation between two or more people, begin a new paragraph each time a new person speaks. Place a phrase identifying the speaker in the paragraph with the speech unless it is obvious who is talking.

"Maybe I can't write like Shakespeare," murmured Hildegard, "but my play deals with important issues."

Ms. Donahue sighed and folded her arms. "I recognize that, dear. I just want to cut some of the longer speeches."

"But that will ruin it!"

"I think," the assistant director interjected, "that cutting some of the dialogue will make it easier for the audience to understand your message."

Go on

Name _____ Date _____

❶ Show What You Know

Add the missing quotation marks to the dialogue below.

Come on, sis, you know that I'm happy to help you most of the time, but when it comes to buying a present for your annoying friend . . . Alex paused and shrugged his shoulders, Well, you're on your own.

She's not annoying. She's just free-spirited.

It's more like she feels free to blab as much as she wants. Besides, he said dismissively, you don't need my help. I wouldn't even know what to get her.

Carla's eyes welled up with tears. But, she said, I just need a ride to the mall!

Well, if that's what you wanted, why didn't you say so, Alex laughed, I'm going there anyway. You can ride along.

✔ Proofreading Power!

Correct the five punctuation errors in the use of quoted material below.

The plays of Elmira Constance Chase deserve to be better known by the public and by the critics. In his biography of Chase, Justin Tarsus says Chase was dedicated to a truthful portrayal on the stage of suburban American families. He goes on to say that Chase drew on her own "Delightful and painful experiences" for her characters and their dilemmas. Noted theater critic George Anderson did not feel that Chase's characters could be drawn from life. He said Her characters are too odd to have been based on real people." Though the debate will continue, it is not the source of Chase's inspiration but the fruits of it that matter.

¶	Indent paragraph
⌃	Add
⊙	Add a period
୶	Delete
≡	Capitalize
/	Make lowercase
∩∪	Reverse

©TIME Inc.

Name _____ Date _____

Apostrophes with Contractions and Possessives

A **contraction** is a shortened version of a word or of two words that often occur together. An **apostrophe** in a contraction takes the place of the dropped letter or letters.

is not ⟶ isn't   could have ⟶ could've

it is ⟶ it's   would not ⟶ wouldn't

● ●

An apostrophe is also used to form possessives. To form the possessive of a singular noun, add an apostrophe and an –s even if the singular noun ends in –s.

Mrs. Wetzel**'s** wrinkled hand strokes the cat**'s** fur.

● ●

To form the possessive of a plural noun that ends in –s, add only an apostrophe.

The muddy dogs**'** tails wagged in unison.

● ●

To form the possessive of a plural noun that does not end in –s, add an apostrophe and an –s.

The **women's** argument ended when the beautiful cat appeared.

● ●

There are four possessive pronouns and four noun-verb contractions that are homophones. In other words, they are pronounced alike, but they have different meanings and are spelled differently. This can be confusing for writers. It will help to remember that a possessive pronoun, unlike a possessive noun, never has an apostrophe.

Possessive Pronouns Versus Contractions				
possessive pronouns:	your	its	their	whose
contractions:	you're	it's	they're	who's

possessive pronoun: **Your** dog could help people in nursing homes.

contraction: **You're** sure to find the experience of helping rewarding.

Go on →

#10132

Name _____ Date _____

❶ Show What You Know

Label each word that has an apostrophe with *sp* if it is a singular possessive noun, *pp* if it is a plural possessive, and *c* if it is a contraction.

Tamisha's dog would be a good candidate for the animal-assisted therapy program. That's

a new program at the assisted-living center in town. I read about it in the newspaper's latest

edition. The center's staff is inviting people and their pets to be trained to participate.

They're sure that the residents will benefit from interaction with friendly animals. Animals'

temperaments can vary greatly, so it'll be important to find animals who are comfortable

with strangers. Their handlers' temperaments must be suitable, too!

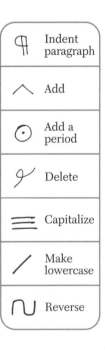

Proofreading Power!

Use the proofreader's marks to correct the 12 errors in the newspaper article below.

The Trumble Center for Assisted Living is looking for friendly and well-behaved pets to participate in they're new animal-assisted therapy program. The centers director, Dr. Crumwell, said, "Health professional's have long been aware that interacting with animals can calm people. Dog's wagging tails and cats purrs let people know that they are accepted just as they are." But not every animal will make a good therapy animal. Dr. Crumwells own dog, for instance, cant tolerate loud noises. The doctor suggests that owners' need to evaluate they're pet's behavior and their ability to tolerate stress. Its important that a therapy animal remain calm, even when poked by a cane, stroked by a trembling hand, or bumped by a residents' wheelchair.

¶	Indent paragraph
∧	Add
⊙	Add a period
♀	Delete
≡	Capitalize
/	Make lowercase
∩∪	Reverse

Name _____   Date _____

Fragments and Run-on Sentences

A **sentence fragment** is not a true sentence. A fragment is grammatically incomplete, lacking a true subject or a true predicate or both. Beware of verbals, words formed from verbs that can be mistaken for the predicate of a sentence.

verbal

Fragment (no predicate): The door <u>swinging</u> in the wind.

The verbal in the above fragment is part of an adjective phrase that modifies the noun. It is not acting as a predicate.

Correction (predicate added): The door swinging in the wind <u>creaked on its hinges</u>.

• •

Often a fragment is a dependent clause beginning with a subordinating conjunction or a relative pronoun. The clause has a subject and verb, but the subordinating conjunction or relative pronoun makes it dependent on its connection to a main clause. A dependent clause needs to be connected to a main clause, which is usually positioned just before or just after the fragment. By correctly connecting the fragment to a main clause, you can create a complex sentence.

Fragment: Although he was afraid. Omar crept close to the mysterious house.

Correction: Although he was afraid**,** Omar crept close to the mysterious house.

Fragment: He heard a strange sound coming from under the porch. Which was in disrepair.

Correction: He heard a strange sound coming from under the porch**,** which was in disrepair.

• •

A **run-on sentence** is two or more independent clauses joined together as if they were one sentence. Sometimes there is no punctuation, and sometimes the writer has used a comma where a period or a semicolon is needed. To correct this problem, separate the sentences into two simple sentences or add a conjunction and correct punctuation to create a compound sentence.

Run-on: Omar saw a cat and three kittens, they were stuck under the porch!

Correction: Omar saw a cat and three kittens. They were stuck under the porch!

Go on

#10132

Grammar, Usage, and Mechanics—Secondary Level   **73**

Name _____ Date _____

❶ Show What You Know

Examine each example below to determine whether it is a run-on, a fragment, or a complete sentence. Write your diagnosis on the line after the example.

Omar decided to rescue the cat and her kittens, the mother cat did not cooperate. _____

She hissed and spit at Omar. Who was just trying to help her. _____

Omar thought that the cat was afraid of people. _____

Proofreading Power!

Use the proofreader's marks to correct the seven errors in the report below.

Feral cats are domestic breed cats. That have been born in the wild. They are usually quite wary of people. Having had no experience with them. A colony of feral cats might develop in a neighborhood. When stray cats have kittens that are never adopted by people. Sometimes, those colonies of cats are fed by animal lovers. Tenderhearted folks who are trying to protect the health of the animals. A hopeful person might attempt to adopt an adult feral cat but often the cat cannot learn to trust its human friends. Although rescuing a litter of feral kittens and socializing them is a challenge too the rescuer's effort is more often successful because kittens have not yet learned to distrust people. Rescuing kittens will help those kittens and it will also help the colony. Which becomes less healthy as it grows larger. Those who are interested in learning more about feral cats should contact their local ASPCA chapter.

¶	Indent paragraph
∧	Add
⊙	Add a period
⌔	Delete
≡	Capitalize
/	Make lowercase
∼	Reverse

Name _____ Date _____

Subject-Verb Agreement

Each sentence you write must have **subject-verb agreement.** This means that the subject of a sentence must agree in number with its verb. Singular subjects take singular verbs; plural subjects take plural verbs.

Singular: The **pot** <u>simmers</u> on the stove. **Plural:** The **pots** <u>simmer</u> on the stove.

Singular: The **potato** <u>is</u> in the oven. **Plural:** The **potatoes** <u>are</u> in the oven.

Note that the suffix *-s* or *-es* is added to most nouns to form the plural, but the same suffix added to regular verbs forms a singular third-person verb.

• •

Do not be confused by words or phrases that fall between a subject and its verb.

The **platter** *holding the fish heads* <u>belongs</u> in the refrigerator.

The **cookbooks** *spotted with grease* <u>are</u> the ones I use most often.

• •

Ordinarily, the number of the subject is not changed by expressions such as *along with, as well as,* or *in addition to.*

Julia, *as well as James,* <u>is</u> a respected cook.

The **onion,** *along with the cloves of garlic,* <u>cooks</u> quickly.

• • • • • • • • • • • • • • • • • • • •

Compound subjects joined by *and* take plural verbs.

Julia and James <u>enjoy</u> cooking on the weekend.

He and I <u>like</u> the smells that fill the kitchen.

For agreement with collective nouns, please see pages 11-12.

• •

Singular subjects joined by *or, either . . . or,* or *neither . . . nor* take a singular verb. The verb should agree with the subject closest to the verb.

Either **Martin** *or* **Ann** <u>fills</u> the dishwasher.

Neither three **fillets** *nor* a **steak** <u>feeds</u> such a large crowd.

• •

An indefinite pronoun refers to an unknown or unspecified noun.

Everyone I know <u>likes</u> ice cream. **It** <u>tastes</u> good.

Some ice cream flavors <u>taste</u> better than others.

Go on

Name _____ Date _____

❶ Show What You Know

In each sentence, underline the subject and circle the verb that agrees with it. Label the subject with _s_ for singular or _p_ for plural.

Special dishes (are/is) associated with holidays and special occasions.

My friend's family (make/makes) a big pot of fish stew to celebrate birthdays.

Either Joseph or his sisters (assemble/assembles) the ingredients.

The pot filled with fish heads, onions, and carrots (bubble/bubbles) in their kitchen.

The mixture of fish and vegetables (create/creates) an intoxicating aroma.

Joseph, as well as his parents and his sisters, (treasure/treasures) the family recipe.

I (have/has) never had the pleasure of tasting this dish.

Proofreading Power!

Correct the 11 errors in the paragraph below using the proofreader's marks.

Not everyone appreciate my family's fish stew, but we loves it. The original recipe were handed down to us by my great-grandparents. My sisters and I talks about how good the stew is, but many of our friends say it's gross. We cooks other dishes in our kitchen, too. Either a turkey or two chickens sits on our dinner table on Thanksgiving Day. A butternut squash, basted with butter and two herbs, go well with the poultry. For special occasions in the summer, burgers or hot dogs sizzles on the grill. Aunt Jane or Aunt Betty mix up some potato salad. My dad's specialty is Boston Baked Beans. He change the recipe every time he makes it. He say cooking is a creative endeavor.

¶	Indent paragraph
⌃	Add
⊙	Add a period
⌿	Delete
☰	Capitalize
/	Make lowercase
∿	Reverse